It's All About 'Who'?

Stories of Purpose and Potential

Dr. Mark T. Grizzard

Contents

Introduction

I grew up in a very small town in Alabama. The community of Reeltown is located between Auburn and Montgomery. Over the past forty years, the community has changed very little. The closest town with a Wal-Mart is Tallassee. Tallassee is a small town with plenty of potential. The Tallapoosa River runs through Tallassee, and a few miles up the river is Lake Martin. Lake Martin is a man-made lake with over 750 miles of shoreline.

What gives Tallassee so much potential is the proximity to the river and the armory alongside the river. Tallassee is home to the last Confederate Armory and only Southern Armory not burned by General Sherman. The Richmond Carbine Factory was moved from Virginia to an old cotton mill in Tallassee during the Civil War, and began manufacturing Confederate carbines. After Sherman and the Union Army burned Atlanta, they began marching west toward Tallassee in hopes of burning the only remaining armory in the South. Somewhere around LaGrange, Georgia, Sherman realized the Union had the war won, and he turned his army around. In the 1980's, the armory was old, but you could go inside and look around. It was in relatively good shape. Some time in the 1990's or maybe the early 2000's. the armory was gutted and the wood removed from the inside. The armory was left to slowly decay in time. Today, the roof of the armory has fallen in, and the area has been restricted. I have often wondered, what if city leaders had preserved the armory and maybe built a river walk. What if they had improved the downtown area, and opened it up for tourism? One can only imagine the potential that Tallassee would have today as a tourist attraction.

Each one of us is full of potential, and we can do one of two things to realize our potential: 1. We can choose not to capitalize on the events and experiences of our past, and in turn limit our growth, or, 2. We can allow the events and experiences of our past to shape who we are and help us progressively grow throughout life. We have had good and bad experiences in life, and sometimes we focus on the bad experiences and allow them to determine and define our lives. You are the sum of both the good and bad in your life. I believe that even bad experiences in life create potential for our future. I struggled for years with alcohol. I don't think I was ever an alcoholic, but I really enjoyed drinking – sometimes too much. In my early years in the military, I was in trouble on several occasions because of drinking. As I look back on those experiences, many were negative and not so pleasant to remember. But then again, I realize that I am the sum of all my experiences both good and bad.

I work with many people who are addicted to drugs and alcohol. I can relate to their addictions because of my struggles in the past. We must come to a point in life where instead of blaming God, or blaming others for our past, we accept personal responsibility and move forward. Does that mean that all the bad experiences in your past are your fault? Not at all. Many people have suffered terrible abuse both physically, emotionally, verbally and/or sexually. Taking responsibility means that you take control of how you think about your past. It's important that we get away from a victim mentality and consider "how" our negative and bad experiences from the past can benefit and help us grow in the future.

I attended Troy State University and after graduating, my family and I moved to Wilmore, Kentucky to attend Asbury Theological Seminary. I had already served eight years in the military, and my past was less than stellar. As a person of faith, I knew that I had been forgiven, but it's not as easy to forget. I remember my first semester at Asbury. The professor asked each student to tell where they were from, and what had brought them to Asbury. I remember students standing up, and sharing their past experiences. One had been the president of his youth group. Another was a preacher's son. I remember one young lady who was the daughter of the Mayor from a large city in New Jersey. As each person stood up, I thought about my own past and how it compared. Honestly, I didn't think there was much comparison. I mean, they had it together. I had been in the military. I had been deployed on several occasions, and I had been in trouble in the military throughout my first four years of service. Although I didn't see it at the time, probably every experience in my life had brought me to that point. There were several good experiences that had helped me to determine what I wanted to do with my future. But there were also several bad experiences that had brought me to a point in life where I wanted to do better. Great experiences have brought you to where you are today – but so have bad experiences. You are the sum of your past. What you choose to do today not only reflects your past but determines your future. God has a purpose for your life, and He has given you the potential to reach that purpose. But at the same time, we have free will. We can choose to live our lives in the past or constantly strive for a better future.

We moved to Wilmore, Kentucky in 1998. My wife, Cindy, had worked several years as a registered nurse at a local Veteran's Administration Hospital and was able to transfer to the Lexington VA. We had sold our furniture and placed our house for sale in Alabama. We then packed up a small trailer, tied our two kids to the top of the car (just kidding), and moved to the bluegrass state. Wilmore is like a holy city. It's a small town with the Asbury campus right in the middle. I was able to find a job working at a homeless shelter in Lexington, KY. Over the next few years, we grew to love Asbury and the surrounding area .

In 2001, I graduated from seminary and was commissioned as a chaplain in the U.S. Army Reserve. A few months after completing seminary, I was attending drill one weekend when I was called by the local police station and asked to come to the jail to talk to three teenagers who had been arrested the night before. When I arrived at the police station, I was taken back to a jail cell where the teenagers were being held. They had been arrested for underage drinking and public intoxication. They were very emotional and wanting to go home. I spoke to them about responsibility while the station prepared their paperwork for release. They were relieved to have someone to talk to and opened their hearts – continually saying how sorry they were for the night before.

As I was leaving the jail, I was called by a member of the Reserve unit who said that a Sergeant had not showed up that morning for drill. His wife had called the unit and asked if someone could go out to see him. As I drove to the Sergeant's house, I reflected on the three teenagers and if and how their lives would change. I thought about how their experiences from the night before would either help or hurt them in the long run. When I pulled in to the Sergeant's driveway, I heard a loud scream and then sobbing. I ran to the house where the Sergeant's wife met me at the door. The Sergeant had just shot himself in the head and was laying on the floor. He had literally shot himself seconds before I knocked on the door, and the young wife had just found him. I was stunned and shocked. I didn't know what to say or how to even begin to comfort the wife or her children. The Sergeant had been battling bouts with depression and had left a suicide note on the stand beside the bed. I stayed at the house for most of the day trying to help the family sort through such a traumatic experience, and left with feelings of anger and despair. I felt inadequate, and I began to question God.

Over the next few weeks, I began to question my call as a chaplain and my reasoning for attending seminary in the first place. I applied to the local police department and decided to step down from the chaplaincy. The following week I was jogging around the campus, and basically arguing with God. I was very angry and bitter, and I didn't understand why things had happened as they did. My thoughts were, "God, you can have this, I'm done". I felt a small voice in my heart say, "Mark, you have always lived life on the edge in the military – you have always pushed the limit. Do you expect that I would call you to live any differently as a Christian?' Being faithful will never be an easy job". It changed the way I thought about myself, about God, and about life in general. Terrible things happen all around us each and every day, but for a person of faith, it's a time and a chance to plant your roots and stand firm. The Apostle Paul did not have a stellar past. Matter of fact, his past was very checkered. He lived in a time and age where terrible things were happening all around him. But Paul never lost sight. He ran the race we call life, and he maintained a trust and a faith in God as His provider, comforter and deliverer. The same is true for you and me.

Don't let your past get in the way of what God wants to do through your future. You have a purpose. Don't let the things that happen around you throw you off course. Keep your focus and run the race. The prize is so well worth it. It's all about Who? Well it's all about God, but God has *you* in mind.

Writing has always been a passion, and I have been meaning to write a book for years. But you know how it is – time seems to get away from us. This past year, I took the plunge. I opened a private marriage and family counseling practice and decided to give writing a shot. As I mentioned earlier, my past is anything but stellar. I don't claim to be an expert on God, the military, counseling, or church. But I know where I've been, and I know that many of those places I never want to return. I have had many great experiences, and a few bad experiences that I wish I could change. But at the same time, I realize that God has brought me through those experiences to make me who I am today. God requires accountability, and I realize today that every decision comes with a consequence – good or bad. It's what you do with the consequences that determines success or failure in life. I can use those negative experiences as an excuse of "why I am like I am today", or I can use both the good and the bad in my past to "make me better than what I am". I choose to try and do the latter. God never promises us that life will be easy, but He does promise us He will take every step with us on the way.

Life is full of mountaintop experiences, and life is also full of valleys.

15

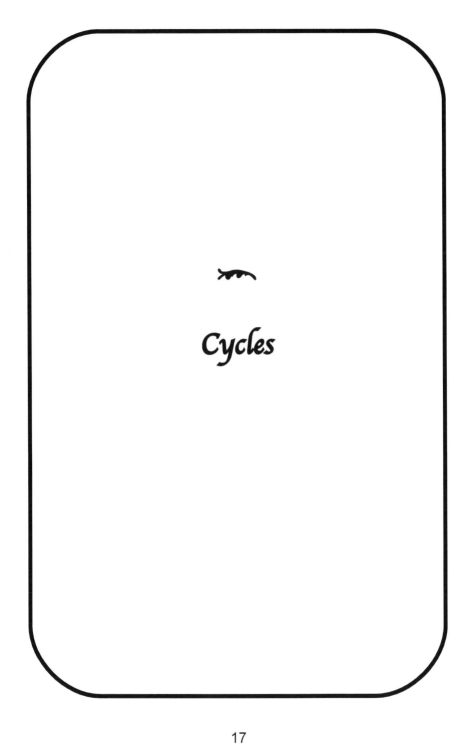

Cycles

Ever wished you had a "do over"? Ever wished you could go back and change something in your past? I do – all the time. My father retired from the Air Force at Keesler Air Force Base, and we moved to Lineville, Alabama for a couple of years. I attended school there through the third grade, and I liked a girl named Sherry. I must have called her every single day because I still remember that phone number 40 years later. After third grade, we moved to a small community about 50 miles away, and I lost contact with Sherry. Eight years later, I was in eleventh grade, and I started thinking about her. Did I say that I had called her so many times in third grade that I had memorized her number? Sherry answered the phone and we talked for a few minutes. Finally, I got up the nerve and said, "Sherry, will you go with me?" "Go where?", Sherry replied. "Well, go steady with me". Sherry says, "Um, Mark, I haven't seen you in like 10 years". I said, "Well, I still look the same". I don't remember her exact reply, but I know it wasn't "yes". I remember hanging up the phone and thinking about how stupid I must have sounded. I couldn't believe I had said to Sherry that I hadn't changed since third grade. Heck, I had put on 100 pounds in muscle and had facial hair. Well, not really, but I had grown quite a bit.

I have wanted a Do-Over on so many occasions in my life. I have spent much of my life looking back. When I first joined the military, I always looked back to the good ole days of high school. When I got out of the military and started college, I thought about those good ole days in the military. Got out of college and went to seminary – yes, you guessed it - I was looking back. I went back in the military and looked back at seminary with a tear in my eye. Now I am out of the military and wish I were still in. Even now, I look back at when our children were young – the good ole days. Those were all good days, but I have to watch myself so that I don't get so absorbed and focused on the past that I forget about the present and the opportunities that God has placed before me for my future. God has a plan for each one of us, but so often, we are so busy looking back that we lose sight of God here and now. Other times, we are so busy planning ahead and looking forward that we forget about how God is working in our present. God has placed you here today for a purpose. It's up to us to find and fulfill that purpose. You can't ever fulfill your purpose if you are constantly looking back. You may say, "Well, Mark, I am too old to have a purpose". I have often told church members that the way you know if God has a purpose for your life is to check your pulse. If you have a pulse, you have a purpose. God isn't finished with you.

I graduated from Troy State University with a degree in Human Resource Management. One of my closest friends was planning on applying to Law School at the University of Alabama. Chris said, "Mark, let's apply for law school together and move our families to Tuscaloosa". I had already made up my mind to attend either law school or seminary, but I felt a stronger pull toward seminary. So we both applied for law school and I also applied at Asbury Theological Seminary. The more Cindy and I thought and prayed about our options, the more we felt sure that Asbury was the place. In the fall of that year, we moved to Wilmore, and I started attending seminary. At the same time, Chris and his family had moved to Tuscaloosa and began classes. We stayed in touch with each other over the years, and Chris graduated from law school the same year I graduated from seminary. Several years later, I was visiting my parents in Alabama when Chris came pulling in to the driveway in a nice BMW. Chris said, "hey dude, jump in – I want to show you something". Chris took me out to his summer home on Lake Martin and opened one of three garage doors. My eyes lit up! In the garage were two very nice Harley Davidson motorcycles. "Chris!!! Please tell me which one is mine!!!!" Chris just laughed as he showed me his motorcycles, his lake home, and his boat.

I remember Chris saying, "Mark, I tried to get you to go to law school with me – we could have gone into practice together". His words hit me like a ton of bricks. I had finished seminary and was an officer in the military, but I had never dreamed of having a Harley Davidson or a lake home. Chris went on to tell me that he had won a large lawsuit for a client which had helped propel his law practice in "to the money". My family and I were driving back home, and I said to Cindy, "maybe I should have gone to law school. We could have a lake home and a BMW". Cindy said, "Mark, you can't go back in the past, so you need to be happy with what you've got in the present". I was thinking "Do-Over" big time, and Cindy is saying "be content". I've got to admit, that meeting with Chris played a head game with me for months. But I slowly began to realize that God had me where I was supposed to be at the right place for the right time. We must be content with who and where we are in life before we can ever be happy in the future.

In Matthew 7:24-27, Matthew says, [24]"Everyone then who hears these words of mine and does them will be like a wise man who built his house on the rock. And the rain fell, and the floods came, and the winds blew and beat on that house, but it did not fall, because it had been founded on the rock. And everyone who hears these words of mine and does not do them will be like a foolish man who built his house on the sand. And the rain fell, and the floods came, and the winds blew and beat against that house, and it fell, and great was the fall of it." Matthew reminds me that when I am always looking back – when I live life going through the same cycle over and over again, I cannot build a house on firm foundation. A strong foundation comes through our faith and how we handle our problems. A firm foundation comes through what we think of our ourselves, how we think of others, and how we think of God. I like to think of the house as my life. My life rests on the foundation that I have laid in the past, and the foundation that I continue to lay in the present. If I want my foundation to be strong in the future, I must be constantly strengthening it today. How do I strengthen my foundation today? I choose to live a life of faith. I choose to believe that God has brought me through both good and bad experiences for a purpose. I choose to believe that God will use each and every experience, both good and bad, to shape my future. And I choose to believe that my future is bright and full of life because I know where I've been and where I'm going. I am a child of God with the faith to know that I am in the palm of his hand. While I know that I will go through storms in life, I also know that God has given me the strength to weather the storm.

I spoke to Chris just the other night to get permission to use his name and this story. Chris is still loaded. I call him "Mr. Greenjeans". He would argue that he is broke and needs a loan, but Chris has done well in life. What amazes me about Chris is that he has always been content with wherever he was in life. I remember how poor we both were in college. Chris was always content. He knew where he was going, but he did not focus on the past or even the future so much – Chris was about "getting through today". Today, he hasn't changed. He is successful in business and in life. But he still lives life focused on the present with the future in mind.

Most people live life in cycles. We repeat the same mistakes which often have the same consequences. Take for instance anger. Anger is not the sin within itself – the Scripture teaches that God has the emotion of anger. But so often anger leads to the mistake of words or actions that we later regret. In return, those words or actions have consequences in that we are hurt or someone else is hurt. I have met people who live life in cycles. They make a mistake, face the consequences, and then tell themselves that they will never make the same mistake again. That's the end of the first cycle. Then you know what happens? They make the same mistake and suffer the consequences, and then tell themselves that they will never make the same mistake again. And the cycles go on and on. I know someone who has a history of talking about people behind their back. She means well, but she just can't help gossiping about others. The mistake was talking about someone behind their back, and the consequence was hurting the person, and that person never wanting to talk to her again. She would think to herself, "I shouldn't have said those things". But instead of learning from those mistakes, she tends to repeat them over and over pushing people away. Today, she doesn't have many friends to reach out to because they have been hurt in one way or another by her actions.

Several years ago I was attending church in Tallassee, Alabama. I remember the young preacher preaching on learning from our mistakes.

He was relatively new to preaching, but he was an excellent preacher. He said there are three types of people – 1. Smart people, 2. Average people, and 3. Not so smart people. Smart people learn from the mistakes of others and apply those mistakes to their own life. Average people learn from their own mistakes and apply those mistakes to their lives. Not so smart people never learn from anyone's mistakes including their own. Living life in cycles tends to ostracize people from your life, and it leads to depression and anxiety.

Our lives are constantly in a state of change. We are born and spend time learning to get around on our own. Before long we are starting school, and hopefully, we progress through the grades and graduate from high school. Many go on to college while others go to work. We open a new chapter when we get married and then another when we have children. Most of us work, so that we are progressing through life hoping to retire one day. Cycles are not bad, but repeating cycles over and over can be bad. What if we kept repeating the toddler stage, or what if we continued to repeat elementary school? It wouldn't be conducive to our growth. To healthily grow and progress through life, we must be willing to embrace change. Change is evident – and we all must learn to accept it. I have worked with hundreds of people who are depressed. For many, depression has slowly progressed in their lives due to living life in cycles – repeating mistakes over and over again. Depression also occurs to those who have an inability to accept change in life.

After getting out of the military a few years ago, I began pastoring a church. Many churches have people in leadership who have no desire or willingness to change. Now I'm not talking about changing Scripture or changing what you believe – I'm talking about nominal change in general. I remember a couple who didn't want a chair moved from behind the pulpit, not so much because it was a nice chair, but because an ancestor had given it to the church years and years before. Another church couple did not want to change anything about the building – even when it was evident there were problems with the ceiling and the ceiling could fall. I loved this couple, and they are wonderful friends; however, they didn't want to replace the roof and ceiling because a grandfather had been the original builder and had installed the ceiling. Some people never want to see change in life because change can bring about the unexpected, but change is a part of life both individually and organizationally.

As I mentioned earlier, Tallassee has a rich history. In the 1700's, it was home to a Creek Indian village called Tuckabatchee. Tuckabatchee was a sprawling village along the Tallapoosa River. There is a story of a warrior named Tecumseh who traveled from Chillicothe to Tuckabatchee. Chillicothe was a Shawnee village located in present day Ohio. Tecumseh came to Tuckabatchee to meet with the chiefs of the Creek nation. Now remember, Tecumseh didn't have a car or even a horse, so he put on his jogging shoes, and legend has it that he jogged from his village in Chillicothe to the Creek village. The distance between the two villages was a mere 700 miles, but Tecumseh had a message to share and he was willing to do what it took to share it. Needless to say, Tecumseh was probably in decent shape. I'm not sure how long it took him to make the trip, but I can imagine at least a day or two. Seriously, probably about a month or so. He met at the Tuckabatchee village, and he told the Creek Indians that all Native American Indians should join forces to fight the "white man". The "white man" was encroaching upon the lands of Native Americans, and Tecumseh had the foresight to see it coming. The problem was that the Creek chiefs didn't think Tecumseh knew what he was talking about.

Some of the leaders were for Tecumseh's proposal while others were against it.

The problem from some of the Creek Indian's point of view was the fact that the Creeks had traditions and a way of life. And their way of life was good – they liked it. I imagine the Creek leaders thought, "we don't want to upset our apple cart – maybe things will stay the way they have always been". The story goes that Tecumseh became angry with the Creek chief's complacency and lack of motivation to join forces, so he gave them a prophecy. Tecumseh basically told them, "Listen, I am going to jog back to the house and when I get there, I am going to stomp my foot and you will feel the earth tremor from it". Tecumseh set off on his journey back home, and something very interesting happened. Several weeks after Tecumseh left Tuckabatchee, the Creek nation felt the earth tremor. I have heard that there actually was a small earthquake in Alabama sometime after Tecumseh's visit. I don't believe it was from Tecumseh stomping his foot, but it's a very interesting coincidence.

Maybe the Creek chiefs didn't listen to Tecumseh because they thought they could defend their lands. Or maybe it was because they just couldn't imagine their way of life ever changing. Whatever the case, there was a sense of complacency to change on the Creek's part. In a sense, their complacency led to their utter defeat by General Andrew Jackson at Horseshoe Bend in present day Dadeville, Alabama. What can we learn from the Creek's response in Tecumseh's day? We can learn that we must be willing to change. Change is normal. Lack of change leads to stagnation and ultimately defeat. Change breaks cycles of complacency in life. In addition, I think God reminds us of change in everyday life.

I believe in Grace. There are many types of grace, but the grace that reminds me of change is Prevenient Grace. Prevenient grace is the grace that God shared upon the world even before you were ever born. It's evident in creation. In other words, God's DNA is all over creation. At some point in life, the normal person is going to wonder about creation. Is there someone or something behind the scenes? Or is everything just coincidence? Think about the sun – how is it that it has continually burned since the beginning of time? Gas normally has a flash affect and burns out rather quickly. When we walk outside, we experience the beauty of nature. Is it a coincidence that the sun warms the earth, the moon gives us light at night, trees give us oxygen, and the atmospheric pressure and oxygen remains exact so that life can be sustained? What about water? What about our body? It's a miraculous piece of work when you consider everything that must work simultaneously for us to function as humans. For me personally, it would take greater faith to believe that there is no God than to believe that a Creator has created and ordered all creation. God teaches us change in life, and God teaches us change through the seasons. Change is not a bad thing. Matter of fact, God intended for it to be a good when He is at the center.

When we fail to learn life's lesson the first time around, life has a way of bringing it around again for a second chance. Take for instance a child. If a child is never taught discipline and respect for authority, chances are that someone or something in time will be the teacher. During my first four years in the military, I spent a lot of time in trouble. Looking back, alcohol was always the common denominator. Normally, we were placed on restriction which meant having to stay in the barracks each day and not being allowed to leave our room. Televisions and radios were removed from our presence. Restriction usually lasted thirty days and it was a long thirty days. In addition to restriction, we were sometimes given thirty days' extra-duty. It would seem that a young, "halfway" smart young man would learn lessons quickly. Not me! At least not at that time!

My first time on restriction was at the age of 19, and yes, it was alcohol related. As a young enlisted military man, you didn't want to attend a party and pass out during the party. That was considered rude and incompetent. A young man named Tommy had recently arrived from basic and advanced training and was assigned to our unit. He was assigned to my squad, and we started indoctrinating him in to the unit. Tommy was from Texas and had grown up riding bulls on a sprawling ranch. We were invited to a party off base one night. I noticed soon after arriving that Tommy was drinking beer as fast as he could "pop" the top. I told him to slow down, but he informed me that he could handle his alcohol and had been drinking since he was 12 years old. Within a half an hour, he started telling everyone how "tough" he was and how no one in their right mind would want to mess with him. Within an hour, Tommy was hollering and screaming something about being from Texas and bull riding. Within an hour and a half, he was OUT. Passing out at a unit party was not a smart move especially for a newbie. Within minutes the black, green and red magic markers were out. Tommy's face was colored from his shoulders to the top of his head. Even his ears and eyelids were colored. Remember the Polaroid Instant Camera? Someone happened to have one and started taking

32

pictures. Tommy never even moved while he was being "fixed up". By the time the guys were finished, Tommy looked like a sick Martian. By that coming Monday, Tommy's face was still black, green and red because the guys had used permanent markers. Poor Tommy was only used to taking one shower per week (just kidding, Tommy☺), but that next day Tommy took four or five showers, and the colors were still there. We thought it was hilarious, but the senior enlisted and officers in our unit didn't think it was quite so funny. As it turned out, everyone in our squad was put on restriction for 30 days including yours truly. By the way, it took Tommy a week to wash the colors off his face.

I remember those long days on restriction, and I remember telling myself that I would never end up in that predicament again. I would love to say that I learned my lesson, but that would be a downright lie. About three weeks after getting off restriction, me and a couple of buddies were riding around on some old county roads near our base, and of course, the common denominator was alcohol again. It was well after dark, and we noticed a young couple parked beside a local lake. The surrounding area was heavily wooded. My friend, Ken, had recently purchased a Halloween werewolf mask. We parked the car about 100 yards away from the couple, and Ken got behind a tree close to their car. As they were walking from the lake to their car, Ken let out a bloodcurdling scream and darted out from behind the tree. He ran directly across the trail and back in to the woods. The woman screamed, but not near as loud as the man. I could hear him cussing even after they were in the car. He went to back out and backed in to a ditch.

Ken ran through the woods and back to the car, and said, "let's go, man, go! The dude backed in to the ditch!". My luck has never been that good when it comes to getting out of trouble. Matter of fact, I am probably the only person that can get a speeding ticket on a dirt road. We cranked the car, and started to head out and got pulled over by a local sheriff's deputy before we had gone a quarter of a mile. At about the same time, the man and woman came running up to the police car telling him what they had just seen. Ken wasn't smart enough to hide the mask – he had it sitting on his lap. The deputy got the mask and showed it to the man. Boy, was he mad, and boy was it a bad experience for us. We found out that he was a Lieutenant Colonel. To make matters worse, we also found out he was on a first date and was very angry because he had "lost his cool" in front of the young woman. We were taken to the security station and our Commander was notified. For us, it was another thirty days on restriction. That year, I spent a total of 60 days on restriction. But I was starting to get it – actions have consequences. For every action – there's a reaction. You can learn from your mistakes, breaking the cycle and moving forward – or you can continue to repeat the same mistakes and continue to receive the same consequences.

The Only Easy Day Was

Yesterday

I had the opportunity to meet some of the military's finest and toughest men. Army Rangers and Green Berets are a special group. Hundreds of young men in great shape wash out of the training each year. The Air Force has their Pararescuemen and Combat Controllers, and it certainly takes a special type of man to complete the training. The Marine Corp has MARSOC. Force Recon Marines are in excellent shape and very professional. The Navy has their Navy Seals. The Seals go through some of the toughest training in the world to include Basic Underwater Demolition and "Drown-proofing". Of all the services mottos, I like the Navy Seals the best. The Navy Seal motto is "the only easy day was yesterday". I have thought about just how true that is in life. We are all faced with problems and struggles. When you consider life, the only easy day was yesterday because it is over – you've gotten past it. When struggle and hardship strike, it's important to focus on the here and now. It's important to focus on today and getting through this day. Don't get stuck in the past, and don't be too quick to look to the future. Focus on this day, maybe this hour, or even this minute. I was talking to a friend who spent eight years as a Navy Seal. He says that in training, would-be Seals must learn to focus on one evolution, or one event, at a time. To focus on the past, or to focus on the future, leads only to doubt in your ability in the present.

I work as an addictions counselor and just recently opened a private Marriage and Family Therapy practice in North Georgia. I work with couples who are struggling in marriage, and I work with many people who are struggling with some form of addiction. Last week, a young man came to my office. I have known Bryan for about three months, and he is always quick to smile with a great personality. He was sexually and physically abused as a child and began using drugs at the age of twelve. It's difficult to understand, but his mother was his supplier. Bryan was an excellent baseball player in high school, but he let drugs steal any possibility of a career. By the time he was 18 years old, he was a drug addict. He is now 29 years old and facing jail time for owing money on child support as well as probation expenses. Bryan was in my office yesterday and said, "Mark, what am I going to do if I go to jail? I won't be able to continue treatment". Bryan and I started talking about foundations. Everything we do today is laying a foundation for our lives tomorrow. If we use drugs today, we are laying a foundation for drug use tomorrow. After a moment of silence, he said, "my foundation is messed up and I'm out of options". The fact is that God has a purpose for Bryan's life even today. It's so easy to give up on the future. We endure trial and hardship, we create debt for ourselves – both physically, mentally, emotionally, and spiritually- and then we start having an "I don't care" attitude. I see people in my practice each week who have basically given up on life. It's so important for us to remember that the only easy day was yesterday. Life brings hardship and struggle, but when we face our struggles head on, we begin to lay a firm foundation. As we overcome each hardship, our foundation grows stronger. 2 Timothy 1:7 says, "For God has not given us a spirit of fear, but of power and of love and of a sound mind". In other words, don't be afraid of hardship and struggle – face your problems head on. God has given you exactly what you need to overcome your struggle today. When we lose hope, we begin to crush the ability of the Spirit of God to work in and through us.

So what about Bryan? He has a terribly cracked foundation. But that doesn't mean that his life is over. Sometimes we must be willing to tear the foundation up to prepare a new one. For Bryan, tearing down the foundation means facing the consequences of his past decisions and being willing to move forward. Bryan is facing six months in jail. It is difficult as a therapist to tell someone they need to go to jail. We believe in hope, and we believe that everyone will get better under the right circumstances. But at the same time, Bryan must face his past to prepare for his future. Does that make sense? In other words, Bryan must hold himself accountable and accept the consequences of his past actions in order to move forward and begin strengthening his foundation.

Many of us never build a strong foundation because we are too busy blaming others for our past. By the end of our session, Bryan said, "maybe these next few months in jail will help me with my foundation". It's important that we look for the positive in every situation. A firm foundation not only affects us, but it affects those who look to us for support. Build strong foundations in life. If you aren't living your dreams, dream another dream. If you have failed in one thing, start something else. Be willing to accept responsibility for your past. But at the same time, don't dwell on it. It's over – It's gone. Learn from your past, and be willing to move forward focusing on the present. It's so easy to get stuck in the past and miss out on the present.

My mom and dad were born in the Great Depression. They talk about how hard times were as children. Dad was just saying the other day how he used to walk along the road looking down just hoping to find a penny. That was back in the days when you only were given one pair of shoes a year, and you could only wear them on Sundays. Dad would have football practice after school each day then have to run (not jog) ten miles home to do his chores. I think parents may sometimes stretch how hard they had it to their children. I know I do to mine. Mom and dad talk about how hard those days were, and how they had to pick cotton as children. I love listening to their stories. But they always talk about those days with affection. I asked dad sometime back if he missed those days. He said, "yea, I do. They were hard days and we were very poor, but we didn't know we were poor". Dad says you didn't have to look out the window when someone came in to the yard, you could just look out one of the cracks in the wall. Heck, I don't think they even had windows back then.

The fact is that times can be hard when we are living in the middle of them, but then we look back and realize that there was some happiness and joy to be found. Don't get me wrong, I don't like hardship and struggle no more than you, but during difficult times, I am reminded of my favorite Scripture in the Bible. 1 Corinthians 10:13 says, "No temptation has overtaken you that is not common to man. God is faithful, and He will not let you be tempted beyond your ability, but with the temptation He will provide the way of escape, that you may be able to endure it". I am also reminded that normally I can find something good even in the bad.

I was talking to a client the other day who was telling me how bitter he was becoming. I asked him why he felt bitter, and he said it was because of all the things happening in the world today. We paused in our counseling session to talk about the danger of harboring bitterness in our lives. Bitterness will almost always lead to a state of depression, and sometimes even anxiety. He asked me if I had ever felt bitter about life in general to which I said, "oh yea, many times in life". But what determines whether that bitterness leads to depression is how you respond to it in the here and now. I personally choose each morning how my day is going to be. I can wake up and talk about how bad it's going to be, or I can wake up and choose to be happy. It's all up to me.

I remember going to basic training in 1986. I had hair down to my shoulders, so dad told me it might be a "wise decision" to get a haircut before I left. My recruiter had told me not to worry about it. He said they would "trim" my hair up a little bit. Dad said, "Son, they are going to shave your head". My reply was, "nah, dad, that was back in your day. The recruiter says they will give me a little trim". When I arrived at basic training and got off the bus, the first person I saw was Staff Sergeant O'Connell. He ran up to me, and after looking me over carefully, asked me what band I had sung in. I was like, "huhhh?". For some reason, he wasn't too fond of the word "huh". He said, "Boy, with that hair, you were either in a rock band, or you on the wrong side of the base". Over the next few minutes, I started getting really nervous because he kept hollering. He wanted to know where I was from and what my "major malfunction" was. The drill instructors marched us in to the medical facility for a urinalysis. The entire time, Staff Sergeant O'Connell was following me screaming something about long hair and women. Six by six we were called in to provide a urine sample. When my name was called, I walked back to the urinal, and no matter how hard

I tried, I couldn't go. I squeezed – I pushed – I closed my eyes and prayed – but nothing was helping. The entire time I was trying, O'Connell was in one ear, and another Drill Sergeant decided that my other ear was getting lonely, so he started yelling in it. Ever had two people screaming in both of your ears? It's sorta confusing to say the least. They kept screaming for me to "GO NOW or you will die!". To make a long story short, I was the last person to urinate in a cup. I was in the clinic for over three hours trying my best to "use it" in the cup. Little did I know at the time, but I had been "earmarked" by the drill sergeants. I had created consequences for myself that evening that would affect me for the weeks to come. By the time I finished and went back outside, the others were waiting (standing at attention) in the parking lot. By the look on their faces, they didn't seem to understand my situation.

I knew for sure that it had to be the worst day of my life. To make matters worse, they marched us over to the barber, and they shaved our heads. Dad was right. It was then that I began to wonder what in the world I was doing there. I had much more important things to be doing back home – riding around Tallassee on Saturday nights, and hanging out with friends.. The next few months were tough, and I honestly didn't want to be there most of the time. But what's so funny is now that I look back, I miss those days. They were actually good days, but I was only looking for the bad. Fast forward 20 years later in my military career. I would often tell young military men and women to enjoy it. I would say, "hey, you are going to look back one day and realize these are good days". But for some reason, they didn't look at their situation the same way I did. It's funny how time changes our perspective on things in life.

No matter what situation you find yourself in, plan for the worse but always expect the best. Don't let setbacks throw you off course. Sometimes you just have to say that "No matter what happens today – this is going to be a good day because I choose to live it with hope and expectation". When things seem to be going bad, always look for the best in the situation. You may say, "Mark, how can you look for the good in all situations?". Honestly speaking, some situations may not have any good to look for. However, every situation can be used in the future to help yourself and others. There are two ways that every situation can have good. First is if you learn from the situation. Second is if you are willing to use your experiences to help or teach others in the future. The key is remembering and learning from your struggles and hardships.

We all go through times of suffering in life – it's a part of life. I have heard preachers say that it's not God's will for anyone to suffer. For me, that sounds so pious. If it were God's will that we never suffer, why did God allow Jesus Christ to suffer? I used to question God because I felt like He was "allowing" me to suffer more than usual. But then one day it dawned on me, if I get angry with God because of my circumstances, could I be elevating myself above Christ Himself? If Christ suffered, then isn't it possible that I may have to suffer in life?

Suffering is a delicate subject to address especially among believers because sometimes we do question God. God, why am I suffering? Why am I so lonely? God, why do I feel so bad? No one wants to suffer. But God does allow suffering, and just like Jesus, it can be a part of His will for us at times. I see a young man named Randy each week. Randy is depressed and rightly so. He served four years in the United States Marine Corp. During those four years, Randy deployed to Iraq two times. Nearing the end of his second deployment, he stepped on an Improvised Explosive Device (IED), and was hospitalized for over a year. The injuries he sustained resulted in losing his right leg above the knee and his left leg below the knee. Randy is only 30 years old and struggles with his handicap as well as Post Traumatic Stress. A few weeks ago, he asked me if it was God's will for him to be handicapped. As a minister and as a therapist how do you respond? No one is a supreme expert on God. My response to Randy was that God does not "cause" suffering, but he "allows" it. He quickly responded with another question, "Why does God allow it then?" Sin has caused depravity in the world we live in. Things like war, sickness, and pain are not God's will, but yes - God will allow it. It goes back to the idea of cycles. We act and there is a reaction. For every decision, there is a consequence throughout our lives. We are living with the consequences from the decisions that we made years ago. We are even living with the consequences, both good and bad, that our parents made decades ago. We face those consequences, and so often others as well as our children are affected. War, sickness, pain and other hardships are consequences from decisions made long ago – starting with Adam and Eve. Most of the alcoholics and drug addicts that I work with have a history of alcoholism and addiction dating back generations. They are facing the consequences from decisions they made, sometimes years before, to drink alcohol or use drugs. In some cases, they may be dealing with consequences even as far back as their parents or grandparent's decision to use drugs or alcohol. Others are dealing with depression issues that date back generations. The most important thing we can do today for our children and for others around us is to work toward physical, mental, emotional and spiritual happiness. It really does mean a lot to others.

The list doesn't end with alcohol and drugs, so don't be too quick to point the finger. Many of us struggle with low self-esteem. We make decisions based on how we feel about ourselves or others, and in turn, others are affected. Our children and those who look up to us learn to make similar decision resulting in similar consequences throughout life. What about negativity? One of the most negative people I have ever met is a middle-aged lady with two children. She always looks for the negative in everyone and everything. I have noticed that her children are becoming just like her. Can you blame them? That's what they have learned and been around their entire lives. So yes, we face the consequences of not only the decision that we have made in the past, but also the decision others have made before us.

So back to the question, does God allow me to suffer? Yes – Yes, He does. But He gives you the strength and the fortitude to come against and overcome every problem, hardship, and struggle. In 2 Corinthians1:8-11, the Scripture teaches us that God often allows "some" to suffer more than "others". Is that possible? Paul says that they were "so utterly burdened beyond our strength that we despaired of life itself". In other words, Paul is saying that times were so difficult that they didn't like "life" in general. Paul continues by saying that "Indeed, we felt that we had received the sentence of death. But that was to make us rely not on ourselves but on God who raises the dead. He delivered us from such a deadly peril, and He will deliver us. On Him we have set our hope that He will deliver us again". The key to overcoming hardship is found in these few verses. The passage says "they were burdened beyond their strength". To be burdened beyond one's strength is to have more than one can handle. The Scripture is saying that, yes, you can have more than you can handle in life. It's absolutely possible! That's why it's so important to have a firm foundation of belief and faith. While you may not be able to handle the suffering, God can and will strengthen you. Where we are weak, He is strong.

Randy confesses to believe in "a" God, but He is not sure what he believes about the God of the Bible. As Randy's therapist, I don't push him. I seek and hope to help him discover who he is and his purpose in life especially since his disability. I present options and even Scripture for him to consider. I asked Randy to read the above passage to me and tell me what he thought it meant. He was somewhat slumped over in his wheelchair, and he began to read slowly. Randy finished the passage, and said, "well, Mark, it sounds like they were stretched thin and couldn't handle anymore". "Every felt like that, Randy?", I asked. "Everyday", was his reply. I think Randy is getting the idea. Sometimes we can't just rely on ourselves. Life wasn't meant to be that way. We need each other, and we need God.

As a Special Operations chaplain, I saw what combat does to men and women. The divorce rate is astronomically high in the military. The suicide rate has continued to rise over the years. Young men and women come back from the horrors of war, and cannot handle the suffering whether it be physical, mental or emotional. The suicide rate in the armed forces has spiraled out of control to the point to where many military care providers are being certified in programs like Applied Suicide Intervention Skills Training (ASIST). Combat veterans come back from war and struggle with life in general. Unless you've been deployed, it's difficult to understand. You go from the adrenaline rush to Hometown, America. Many veteran's cope with the change through alcohol and drugs. Others are prescribed medications from combat injuries and return home addicted. For veterans and civilians alike, it is important to realize that struggles will come, but we must have faith in something or someone. For me personally, I chose to have faith in Jesus Christ. He is my comforter and healer. I have seen my share of suffering over the years, but I have also witnessed faith first hand. And I try to constantly remember that the only easy day was yesterday. Let's focus on today!

The Power of Potential

During my first tour in the military, I lived in the barracks. The barracks had four beds to each room with one bathroom dividing two rooms. It was quite crowded when four people were assigned to the room, and tempers often flared. I had been in the barracks for about six months when a young man named Kim checked in and was assigned to my room. Kim wasn't his real name. He was from Thailand, and it wasn't possible for someone from Alabama to pronounce his first or last name. I just called him Kim. He might have weighed 125 pounds soaking wet. I never saw him eat anything other than rice, or drink anything other than water. I had just turned 21 years old and remember asking Kim, "Man, don't you know that water is bad for you? Look in the refrigerator and grab you a Miller Lite". He just looked at me and shook his head. Kim had come to the United States when he was 12 years old. He spoke decent English, but he couldn't understand decent English, or so I thought. I was from LA, and probably had a little accent. No, not Los Angeles - Lower Alabama. Kim just looked at me funny when I said something he didn't understand. Over the next few weeks, we became good friends. He was a guy who would always follow through on everything he said. But Kim had a problem – he had a difficult time with the other guys. A lot of guys picked on him unmercifully. He had been given the nickname "stick" around the unit because he was so small. The guys would say something to Kim, and he would just smile. I never saw him get angry. We had a senior Non Commissioned Officer (NCO) who constantly ridiculed Kim. He told Kim that he would never amount to anything – that he was a loser. As always, Kim just smiled pleasantly and went about his business.

Well, Kim went to the dental clinic one day and came back sporting a new set of braces. Maybe it was just me, but the dentist didn't seem to have done a very good job putting them on. The braces protruded out of Kim's mouth, and when he tried to close his mouth, it made his lips pucker out. With those new braces, I knew Kim was going to have a difficult time at work, so I decided to watch out after him and try and stop the guys from picking on him. Kim got his braces on a Friday, and he stayed in the room all weekend. I was in and out most of the weekend, but I remember coming in on Sunday evening. Kim was standing with his back against the wall, right ankle in hand, and right toe touching the ceiling above his head. I thought something was wrong, and I said, "Whoa, Kim, what in the heck are you doing?" It was hurting me to watch him. Kim said, "stretching out a little bit". A little bit? Ok! Kim stretched for a few minutes then started "working out". I was laying on my bunk watching him punch and kick the air. The guy was completely focused. I don't remember what I was thinking, but I remember being very impressed. Kim had hung a string tied to a nerf basketball from the ceiling. It was hanging down to where the nerf ball was approximately six feet off the ground. Kim was kicking the nerf ball as he worked out.

I quickly made a mental not to make Kim mad, and after pulling my jaw off the floor, I said, "Kim, are you, umm, like some karate expert?" Kim didn't say anything, and I kept pressing him. "Come on, man, tell me where you learned this stuff". He finally admitted that he was a blackbelt in a martial arts style called Muay Thai. I don't know much about Muay Thai other than knowing to stay away from folks who use it. It's some bad stuff! I told Kim I was a master at "Run-Thai". In other words, if he broke out the "thai" on me, I was going to break out the "run" on him. Later, I learned that Kim's father had been a part of Thailand's Queen's Cobras regiment, and had served in the Vietnam War. The Queen's Cobras were some really bad dudes. I went to work the next day, and I told some of the guys that they better not mess with Kim. I told them that he was one bad dude, and I didn't want to see him get angry. They just laughed it off and continued to pick on him each day. I never saw Kim lose his cool or ever say anything back. He would just smile, shake his head, and walk off. Some of the guys thought he was afraid. I promise you that was not the case. As I got to know Kim over the coming year and heard his stories of immigrating to America, I quickly realized that Kim was far from being a coward – he just wanted peace and tranquility. That's what his life was about.

After about a year, Kim received orders transferring him to another base. I remember our senior NCO saying, "ole Kim, why in the world did he ever come in the military. He should be selling hotdogs on the corner". No one ever thought Kim had any potential. He was always given the less popular jobs when it came to duty, but he always went about his work never complaining. No one ever thought Kim would amount to much. I did. I knew there were seeds of greatness within him.

60

About eight years ago, I signed up for a Facebook account. I started connecting to many of my old military buddies, and you guessed it, Kim and I connected on Facebook. He messaged me one day and said, "Hey Mark, remember me?" I realized within seconds who he was and asked him how he was doing. Guess what Kim is doing now? He's an Oncologist. Not only is he a cancer doctor, but he has worked on a team for years that is researching possible cures for cancer. He lives in California and has patients from all over the world that come to him for surgery and medical advice. Not only does Kim have a medical degree, but he also has a Master's in Business Administration. I can't say I am surprised. I knew Kim when we were 20. He was very smart then - it's just that most people never wanted to hear what he had to say. Now, thousands want to hear him. I wonder what our old NCO would say. I don't think he would still believe that Kim needs to be selling hotdogs on the sidewalk somewhere.

That's the thing about potential. You can't see it, but it's there. It's there in you and in me. It lies dormant, sometimes for years. According to the dictionary, potential is showing the capacity to develop in to something in the future. Notice the word develop. Potential is not just automatically there. It takes time to *develop, to hone, to sharpen.*

Developing potential takes patience, and it will always require hard work. Take Kim for instance, that potential was there even when we were living in the barracks, but it took time for it to be realized. The military was a part of the foundation building process. Kim said that when people laughed and teased him, it just made him want it more. That's the difference between someone who realizes their potential and someone who never does. The person who taps in to their potential is willing to take the insults, they are willing to be laughed at, and they are willing to be ridiculed. They are willing to take risks because they know that through great risks come great rewards. You can't sidetrack them, because they are like a bird dog on point. They set goals, and they will do anything to reach them. Fulfilling your potential has a lot to do with how you view yourself.

You remember the story of Moses? Moses led the Israelites out of slavery in Egypt. After their departure, the Pharaoh sent his army to recapture and bring them back in to captivity. The Israelites were at the Red Sea, and they looked back only to see Pharaoh's army closing in. But you know what God did? He parted the Red Sea. Moses lifted his hand, and the Red Sea was parted. Too easy right? The Israelites passed to the opposite side, and then when Pharaoh's army tried to cross, the walls of water broke and the army was destroyed. I can just hear the Israelites saying, "WOW, God! Awesome!" But do you know what happened? They soon forgot, and they wondered around in the wilderness for forty years looking for the land that God had promised them.

I am reminded of the United States. Our nation has witnessed the power and blessings of God for over 200 years. We are a sovereign nation, and one nation under God. But just like the Israelites, we seem to have forgotten. We seem to be wondering around in the wilderness. We don't know who or what to believe, and it seems that each generation falls just a little further away from God. The Scripture promises us a "land flowing with milk and honey". My favorite Scripture is found in 2 Chronicles 7:14. The Scripture says, "If my people, which are called by may name, shall humble themselves, and pray, and seek my face, and turn from their wicked ways; then will I hear from heaven, and will forgive their sin, and will heal their land". The Scripture is telling us that we must act. I have heard people say, "Faith is not about action". I strongly disagree. I cannot find a story in the Bible about faith and inaction. Faith demands action. Getting back to the story of Moses.

Moses died, and a man named Joshua had taken over as the leader of God's people. Do you remember what happened next? The Israelites found themselves in a similar situation. This time they were on the banks of the Jordan River. The river was at flood stage and very dangerous to cross. Most of the Israelites wanted to just turn around and go back to the wilderness. I mean, can you blame them? They had heard there were giants in the promised land. I imagine they were thinking, "If the river doesn't kill us, the giants certainly will". Honestly, I can't blame them for wanting to go back to the wilderness. I mean, think about it. Over the past forty years, the wilderness had become their home, and they were comfortable there. They had gotten married and given birth to their children there. They had even buried their parents in the wilderness. Yes, it was home. Frankly speaking, when a generation grows up never hearing about the power and blessings of God, they tend to want to choose the wilderness over the promised land. And can you blame them? All they have ever known is the wilderness.

God told Joshua to tell the people to "consecrate themselves – for tomorrow God will do mighty things before you". In other words, Joshua was telling the people to "get ready – God is about to do something big". I think God wants us to be like the Israelites –

constantly preparing ourselves for Him to show up in our lives. Continually building our faith and expecting big things in our lives. God tells Joshua to tell the people that when the feet of the priests who are carrying the Ark of the Covenant touch the water, the water will be parted. Notice the difference? At the Red Sea, God did it all. The people sat back and watched. But the Jordan is different. The people had to "do something". They had to be willing to "get their feet wet". Ever heard the phrase, "you gotta get your feet wet"? That's where the phrase comes from.

So the priest who were carrying the Ark step in to the water, and the water is parted. The Israelites cross over in the Promised Land, and they live happily ever after….Right? Not quite! They had inherited God's promise and they were fulfilling the potential that God had placed in them, but the story doesn't end there. The Scripture goes on to talk about barriers and walls that seem to continually pop up to test their faith. God has a place for you as well. It's a place of promise, and it's something that only you can do. But guess what? There will be giants and walls along the way, and you can't give up. Stay focused knowing that you must "get your feet wet" throughout life in order to move in to the promised land – the place where God has called you to be. God has given you the potential, but you have to make the move.

As a former chaplain and pastor, and today in private practice, I meet people every day who don't realize they have the potential to do some really amazing things. Many people have dreamed a dream, and it died. And honestly, they have mentally and emotionally died with it. Everyone has the potential to fulfill a purpose, and I believe every life has a purpose. Now finding that purpose is another subject matter that will be discussed in another chapter, but everyone has the potential to do something great. That potential lies within. It's lying there waiting to be unleashed. Under the right conditions and circumstances, your potential can become a tidal wave and create opportunity throughout your life.

Have you ever thought about the potential of an apple seed? As I hold an apple seed in the palm of my hand, it weighs nearly nothing. It looks like a dark small speck in the center of my palm. But with the right circumstances and under the right conditions, the apple seed has the potential to become an apple orchard. It can literally produce millions of apples. What are the right conditions and the right circumstances? Well, first it must be planted in good soil, right? It has to be in soil where it can be fed, and where it can grow. Then it must have good water to stay healthy. It's going to also need sunlight. If several conditions are met, that seed is going to become a strong tree and produce good fruit. In time, and if the conditions continue to be met, that tree will produce an orchard. Some trees will grow and produce good fruit while others may catch disease, wither, and die. Others may die due to a lack of water or sunlight. We are much like the apple seed. Alone, we are small and weak. But when the right circumstances and conditions are met, we have the potential to become great – to produce good fruit – and to even affect the lives of others now and in the future.

Ok, here's where it may start sounding weird. Did you now that your potential is related to God's potential? I know it sounds new age, but it's true. Matthew 17:20 says that Jesus replied, "Truly I tell you, if you have faith as small as a mustard seed, you can say to this mountain, 'Move from here to there,' and it will move. Nothing will be impossible to you". Now don't get me wrong, by no means are we equal. God is the creator and the sustainer of life. But God has placed within us seeds full of potential. According to Matthew there is one prerequisite to fulfilling your potential, and that is faith.

I recently heard a joke about a young politician from Washington D.C. who travels to Georgia to go duck hunting. He is out in the field on his first hunt when he shot a duck. The duck lands over in an adjacent field. The politician starts to walk over to retrieve the duck, and as he is crossing the fence, an old farmer on a tractor comes driving up. The farmer says, "young man, what do you think you are doing?" The politician who was cocky and maybe somewhat arrogant said, "I just shot a duck and I'm going to get it". The farmer replies, "uh, I don't think so, this is my land. You need to pay attention to the 'no trespassing' signs posted". This makes the politician mad, so he says, "old man, do you realize who I am? I am a politician from Washington D.C., and I am a man of power. Now drag your old behind out of the way because I am getting my duck!" Well, the old man just scratches his head, and says, "son, that's not how we do things in Georgia. Around here, we go by the three strikes you are out rule. See, I hit you three times then you hit me three times, and it continues until someone gives up". The young politician thought this sounded fair. I mean, he was young and buff, and the old farmer was frail and skinny. So, the young man says, "Ok, old man, you're on!" The old man says "I go first", and he gets off the tractor. The old man stomps on the young politician's toe. Right as the politician started hopping around in pain, the old farmer kicks him in the shin. The politician doubles over and grabs his shin. The old farmer then kicks him in the behind, and the politician falls over. He lays there for just a second, shakes and clears his head, then slowly rises. "Alright, old man, now it's my turn", says the politician as he smiles and rubs his hands together to which the old farmer replies, "Nah, I give up. You can have the duck".

Abraham Lincoln once said, "And in the end, it's not the years in your life that counts, it's the life in your years". I don't want to just live the years through my life – I want to live the 'life' through my years. I want to be able to look back one day, and tell my children and myself that I lived the best that I could. I want to tell them that I was able to accomplish something for them, for myself, and for God. I want to know that my life meant something. No, I wasn't perfect, but I tried. I ran the race to the best of my ability. You can never realize your potential if you are constantly beating yourself up or getting beat up.

So how do we realize and fulfill our potential? How do we reach deep within ourselves and uncover those seeds of greatness that is in each one of us?

First, you must know your source.

What is our source? Our source is God. It is not a mere coincidence that you are able to breath, touch, taste, feel, and see. There is brilliance behind life. A young man was saying just this past week how he didn't believe in God. He reasoned that if there was a God, there wouldn't be so much pain and suffering in the world today. I am not one to judge, and I never try to "hammer" my beliefs into others. I like the analogy of a picture hanging on the wall. If I asked you who painted it, you may say you don't know. But I bet you wouldn't say, "well, Mark, no one painted it. It just somehow got there". Creation is like a beautiful picture, and God is the painter. Personally, I think it's ridiculous to say that the picture of creation and life has no author or no painter. It just wouldn't make sense. For me, it would take more faith to believe that there was no God than to believe that there is a God.

So we must know our source, and our source is God. God is the creator of potential. He has placed the potential within you and has called you for a specific purpose. Going back to the idea that our potential is related to God's potential. Think about it. All things have the same components as the source from which they come, right? I

70

mean, when you take a piece of wood to build a house, you would want to use strong wood. The wood would have the same component as the tree from which it was cut. If the tree was strong, the wood would be strong. So you build a house with strong wood because you want a strong house – one that will withstand the wind and storms. If you chose rotten wood, and built a house out of rotten wood, your house wouldn't be too strong. If a piece of wood has termites, you are not going to use it to build your house because then you would have a house full of termites. The same is true in life. We are like the wood in comparison to God the tree. We have the capability to be strong because He is strong. If we believe the Scripture about the mustard seed, then we realize that it is God who works through our faith, and although we are weak, he is strong. So in turn, we can be strong when He works through us. We have many of the same components as God. We have the component of love. We want to care for one another. We have the component of mercy and compassion, and we have the component of anger, don't we?

We are made with the ability to create. I mean, we have creative minds and we have the ability to destroy. We can destroy someone just with our words. We have the ability to share and we have the ability to take away. God is our source, and we have many of His components to become more like Christ. So often, when all hell breaks loose, we have a tendency to forget the obvious – who and who's we are. Now there's a second part to realizing your potential. Remember, first you must know your source.

Second, you must be maintained by your source.

I believe that when we commit our lives to Christ, we receive a lifetime warranty. I know that some denominations believe that you can lose your salvation while others believe that you cannot. I am not going to try and argue one point over the other. But we are born innocent. As a newborn child, we are closer to God than we ever will be during life. We are sinless – at least for a time. When we give our lives to Christ, He promises that He will be with us here in our physical life, and that one day we will be with Him in eternal life. It's a lifetime warranty. But that warranty comes with an instruction manual. It's call the Bible.

I have always loved motorcycles ever since I can remember. I have one today, and I love riding. When I was twelve years old, I talked my parents into buying me a Yamaha Enduro 100. Boy, I loved that bike. When we bought it, it had a one year warranty. I had the bike about six months, and it broke down. I asked dad to take it to the Yamaha

72

dealership to get it fixed, but he was busy, and we just never got around to it. One day, I decided I was going to fix it myself. So I pull out my dad's tools and commenced to breaking the engine down. I set cardboard and plastic down in the carport because I wanted to put each piece of the engine in a specific area, so I would remember how to get it back together. I know, I know. Stupid right? I did mention earlier that I am "half way smart". Well, I broke the engine down like a professional. Man, I was thinking how good I was doing. But then I ran in to a problem. I couldn't figure out how to get it back together. I worked and worked, and ended up putting the pieces in a box. I talked my brother-in-law to taking it to the Yamaha dealership and guess what? The good thing was the bike was under warranty. The bad thing was that I had voided the warranty by trying to "fix" it myself.

Christians are similar. We know our source is God, but sometimes we begin to try and do things on our own. Or maybe we try to go to others sources for answers and help, and our lives become more chaotic. Whatever God creates must be maintained by its source. Plants that are pulled from their source, grow weak and die. Animals taken out of their environment will grow weak and die. What about fish? Fish taken out of their environment will grow weak and die. And when we remove ourselves from our source, God, we become weak and we spiritually die. God has designed everything to fulfill its purpose. Fulfilling your purpose doesn't mean that you can't have any failures in your past. Matter of fact, it means that you will probably have quite a bit of failure, but it also means that you have learned to get past those failures and start over. God has you right here and right now for a purpose – successes and failures combined!

It's All in the Attitude

I was stationed at Cecil Field, FL during my first tour in the military. Cecil Field was a small base in Jacksonville, Florida. It closed in the early 90's, and today is the home to several reserve units and civilian employers. Back when Cecil was open, there was an enlisted club on base called the Beacon Club. We called it the "Freakin' Beacon". Every chance we got, we went to the Beacon. There was a bar with a dance floor, a game room, and a pizza parlor. One day, I was sitting in the pizza parlor with several of my buddies having a pizza. A young man came walking in and ordered a pitcher of beer and a pepperoni pizza. This guy looked to be about thirty years old, and he walked with a purpose. He wasn't a big guy at all. He may have weighed 175 pounds, but you could tell he was in great shape. He had an "attitude" just by the way he carried himself. I don't mean a bad attitude – more an attitude of self-confidence. I had never seen him before, but he sat down in a booth with his back to the corner and started eating his pizza. A few minutes later, a big Marine came walking in to the pizza parlor looking around. He was a pretty good sized fellow – well over six feet and probably weighing around 240. The Marine spotted this guy in the corner and walked over to him. I could tell he was angry just by the look on his face. The Marine bent down and put both hands on the table. He leaned over and said something to the young man. I couldn't hear what he said, but again, you could tell something wasn't quite right. A few seconds later, the Marine bellows, "I am going to kick your behind right now!". Actually, that wasn't exactly how he said it, but I am trying to keep this clean. The young man in the corner never looked up – he just kept eating his pizza and sipping on his beer. The Marine kept staring at him, and finally picked the picture of beer up and poured it on the young man's head. We were like, "UH OH". It was like being on the sidelines at the Super Bowl. The young man wiped his face with his napkin, and just sort of nodded toward the door saying, "let's go".

Well, I told my buddies, "hey guys, we better go out here and make sure this Marine doesn't kill this guy". We got up and began to follow them toward the door. We couldn't have been over 30 seconds behind them. As I was walking down the hall in the Beacon, I saw them go out the back door, and I saw the door close behind them. Within seconds, we were at the door and going outside. You won't believe what we saw. The big Marine was laying on the ground – I could hear him moaning and groaning, but he was "Down For The Count". A few minutes later, the Military Police arrived on the scene and began asking questions. We didn't see what happened, so we just told them what we knew and went back to the parlor.

About a week later, I saw this young man sitting at the bar in the Beacon Club drinking a beer. I went up to the bar and sat down in the seat right next to him. A few minutes later, I said, "hey man, I am not the police. But I was in the pizza parlor last week, and you are the guy that whipped up on that Marine". He just looks at me briefly, and takes a swig of his beer. I guess I was a little nosy, so I kept pressing the issue. "Hey man, what did you do to that dude – you put it on him didn't ya?" He still didn't say a word. By now, I was starting to get upset and was thinking about pouring his beer on his head. Of course I wasn't going to get past the thinking side of it. Finally I said, "what unit are you with?" He says, "I am on the Seal Teams". Now like I said earlier, the Seals are the Navy's special operations and very good at what they do. Some time later, I heard someone say that members of the Navy's Seal Team Six had been in the area for a few weeks. Seal Team Six are the best of the

Navy Seals. You know what else I heard? The entire disturbance was a mistake – it was a case of mistaken identity. The Marine had seen someone sitting on his car earlier, and somehow thought it was the young man in the pizza parlor. I learned something that day – never go in to a situation physically, mentally or emotionally until you know who or what it is you are coming against.

Confidence is very important if you are ever going to realize your potential. Confidence is a part of attitude, and it determines how you see things around you. Your attitude is what you determine it will be each morning when you get up. You can get out of the bed and think how terrible your day is going to be. Or you can get out of the bed thankful that you have been given another day. Many of you have been through terrible experiences in life, and sometimes it seems impossible to find a positive in such a negative situation. But that's the difference when it comes to realizing our potential. We must be able to look at the past all the while acknowledging the good and the bad. What determines whether you reach your potential is how you respond to those experiences. Acknowledge the bad, but let it strengthen you and help you grow.

One of my favorite teachers in high school was Mrs. Cherry Harris. Mrs. Harris is retired today, but she taught Algebra back in the day. I wasn't the best student in high school, but I can't say I ever really tried. Honestly, I didn't really see the importance of learning Algebra, or doing well in school for that matter. My plan was to join the military, and I knew I just needed to somehow get a high school diploma. To give you an idea of my philosophy at the time, Dad used to say, "why can't you make 'A's, son?" I would say, "Dad, what's the difference in a 65 and a 100? They are both passing." Well, back to Algebra. Halfway through the first semester, Mrs. Harris gave us our averages. Actually, I was probably proud of mine. It was a 55. Mrs. Harris stopped me after class one day and said, "Mark, you know what your problem is?" I don't remember if I tried to guess the answer for extra credit or just shrugged my shoulders, but Mrs. Harris went on to say, "You could be an 'A' student, but you've got to realize you can do it, and you must want to make an 'A'". I doubt Mrs. Harris remembers that conversation, but I never forgot it. I don't remember if I passed Algebra that semester, but I did somehow manage to pass eleventh and twelfth grade and graduate.

I entered the military after high school graduation and served several years. When my first contract was over, I decided to move back to

Alabama to attend college. I had qualified for the Montgomery GI Bill while on active duty. The GI Bill was a great program that paid so much money per month toward education and living expenses. Looking back, I really didn't think I would be able to complete a bachelor's degree. I just wanted to draw the money each month and have a good time. The first semester in college, I registered for weightlifting, basketball, cross country, and history. After the first semester, I made the honor roll. Pretty impressive, huh? That was the first time I had ever had such a high average. So the next semester I took tennis, health fitness, and another really easy elective course. And the second semester I made all "A's" again. By this time, I was really starting to like going to college. By the third semester, the Veteran's Representative and Admissions Counselor called me in to the office and told me that I would need to start taking some foundational courses. To continue to receive the GI Bill, a veteran is supposed to be "working toward" a degree. I had already taken all of my elective courses by the end of the first year.

I figured my college days were soon to be over. I was sweating taking College Algebra, English Composition, Literature, Biology. Just put it like this – I was sweating taking anything that required a book. I remember thinking about what Mrs. Harris had said in high school.

"Mark, you are an "A" student, you just have to realize it and want it".

Mrs. Harris was right on. It is all about attitude and believing in yourself. Over the next few semesters, I took College Algebra, English Composition, Literature, Biology and a couple of years later, finished my bachelor's degree in Human Resource Management. My attitude had changed, and I had begun to believe that maybe I could do well in school. Over the next few years, I ended up earning two Master's degrees and a doctorate degree. Mrs. Harris – you may not remember, but I will never forget. Thank you!

Fulfilling your potential requires having the right attitude, and having the right attitude requires thinking positive thoughts and speaking positive words. James 3:9-10 says, "With the tongue we praise our Lord and father, and with it we curse men, who have been made in God's likeness. Out of the same mouth comes praising and cursing..." James knew the power of attitude, and he knew the power of the tongue. A positive person does not refuse to recognize the negative, but they do refuse to dwell on it. I know people who can and will find negative in everything. But when you are always looking for the negative, that's what you will always find. Some of us have grown up and spent most of our lives around negativity. To move forward and fulfill your potential, you must be willing and able to identify the negative influences in your life. Recognize it, but never dwell on it.

I served as a chaplain in the 919th Special Operations Wing in Florida. We had Air Force Pararescue and Combat Controllers assigned to our Wing. They are some of the most highly trained men in the world. Pararescuemen are trained to parachute out of airplanes at 30,000 feet behind enemy lines. They are experts in weapons and survival. There motto is "So that others may live". They are trained to go behind enemy lines – fighting if need be – and rescue men and women. They are trained in healthcare, triage and trauma. Combat Controllers are trained in survival, but they specialize in all aspects of air-ground communication including air-traffic control and fire support. Basically, combat controllers can provide air traffic control from even hostile areas. Several years ago, I had the opportunity to follow several men through what is known as the "pipeline" for training. It is brutal training to say the least, and trainees are pushed to the very limits of human endurance and stamina.

Pipeline training is almost two years long. Statistics show that only 15-20 percent of the young men who start will actually finish. Now remember, these young men are in excellent shape and must be selected to even begin training. But only about 15 out of 100 who begin the training will finish. I have actually heard guys who have finished the training say you have to "want it more than you want to breath". Trainees spend a lot of time in a pool and must survive what is called "drown-proofing" and "buddy breathing". You can look it up on the internet for more information, but it is really tough training. So why is it that only about 15-20 percent will finish? Why do so many fail? It's all in the attitude. Those who make it see the negative and the pain in training each and every day, but they will not dwell on it. Graduates will tell you that you have to stay focused. If you start thinking about the negative, you will quit.

The reason people get involved with drugs, alcohol, gossip, premarital sex, etc. is because they began to focus on negative thoughts maybe about themselves, or others, or maybe God. And instead of instantly pushing those negative thoughts out of their mind, they started dwelling on them. God didn't create you to be negative – He created you to be positive. Thoughts are very powerful. Your thoughts can "make you", and they can "break you". But you know what else is just as powerful? Your words – Your words can make or break. I want you to remember today, your words have the power to bless and your words have the power to curse. Let me give you an example.

I have two really good friends today. Both were given similar opportunities growing up. They both graduated from high school in the same year, and matter of fact, their birthdays are only three days a part. One friend had a father who was always encouraging him. I would go over to his house, and his father would be telling us how we could be anything we wanted to be. "Just put your mind to it", he would say. His father always encouraged him in school and was constantly building him up mentally. The other friend had a father who was the complete opposite. He was very negative. According to his father, my friend could never do anything right. As a way to ridicule him, his father was constantly calling him, "Einstein". No matter what my friend did, it was never good enough. His father was constantly reminding him how he didn't measure up.

Fast forward twenty five years. The friend with the positive father went on to college and later became a medical doctor. He married a wonderful woman, and they have three sons. He is a great father and is always encouraging his three sons. They are very active in church and in helping in the community. On the other hand, my friend with the negative father has had a difficult life. He quit college after two semesters because of drugs. Over the years, he became an alcoholic and struggled with jobs. He has been married several times and has four children. He is a very negative person and is often very negative to his children.

Two guys with the same opportunities, almost the same exact age, and in the same grade. But the two guys are so different today. Why is that? It's because of the power of the attitude and words that were spoken over them many years ago. Your words have the power to bless, and they have the power to curse. We often don't realize it, but our words have the power to empower and they have the power to destroy. Think about my two friends. The words spoken over them 25 years ago still have power in their lives. And the same is true for us. Our words have power sometimes for generations to come. Now listen to me. Your words and your attitude don't just have power over others - They also have power over you. If you think you don't have a chance, then you probably don't. God has given you the gifts and abilities to do something great, but if you are always down on yourself, you won't ever be able to realize or begin seeing that greatness.

I remember reading about a man who was always expecting the worst. He purchased a ticket to travel on a boat from England to the United States. He was a poor man, and he spent many months saving for the ticket to start his new life. Now the trip was going to take several weeks, so the man went out and bought cans of food and crackers. He bought cans of sardines, potted meat, and pork and beans. Once on board, all the other passengers went to the large dining room to eat wonderful meals, but the man sat at the table in his small room and ate his canned food. Every meal was the same thing. He heard the people in the dining facility talking and could even smell the delicious food, but he continued to eat every meal in his room. The man thought about how nice it would be to join the others, but he didn't have any extra money to spare. He laid in bed each night just thinking about how good a hot meal would taste. The day before the ship was to arrive in the United States, a man approached him and said, "Sir, I cannot help but notice that you are always in your room eating canned food. Why haven't you ever eaten any of the meals cooked in the dining room?". The travelers face flushed with embarrassment. "To tell the truth, I don't have any extra money for food", he said. The other man raised his eyebrows in surprise and said,

"Sir, don't you realize that the meals are included in the cost of the ticket?".

And the same is true in our lives. Jesus Christ has already bought and paid for everything that is good and lasting in your life. But you must be willing to look around and see it. I understand that some of us don't always have a lot of "positive" in our lives, but you can't ever be happy until you start finding the positive in your situation. Listen, our problems remain problems until we make up our mind to do something about them. Sometimes it's difficult, but it's doable. If you can't find the positive in a situation, go out and look for it.

The Power of Purpose

I learned very quickly in the ministry that the key to church growth is purpose. Not only must the church have a purpose, but it must instill in her members a sense of purpose as well. I have pastored several churches over the years. One of the first churches I had the opportunity to pastor was a small church in a rural area. We had a wonderful facility and wonderful people attending, but no one really wanted to do anything. It seemed like every "church" responsibility was left up to the pastor. As long as we held services on Sunday morning, everyone was happy. At a leadership meeting one evening, I shared an idea with the church board. I wanted to begin small groups in the church, but I also wanted to ask each member to be involved in a ministry within the church. In addition, I thought we should ask people who wanted to join the church where they wanted to "plug in" to ministry. One of the elders in the church looked at me over the rim of his glasses and said, "Pastor, are you thinking about trying to get people to do something in the church when they join? People are already busy, and if we do that, no one will join." I asked the board to give it a shot, and if it didn't seem to work, we would stop. Do you know what? It started to work. When someone would ask about joining the church, we would ask them where they felt like plugging in to ministry. Normally, they were more than happy to tell us their passion for ministry. We did have a few who said they didn't want to do anything, and for those people, we politely asked them to continue coming to worship services but to continue to pray about where God would have them plug in. The Church is the Body, and every member is like a cell in the body with a function and purpose for being.

I realize that many pastors would never want to try this, and I can understand. But for us it worked. The church started to grow, and people became very active in ministry in the church and in the community. I think this is a Biblical model not only for the church but for life as well. If the Church is the Body of Christ, and if each member is a part of the Body, then each member must be working toward a common goal and mission. In the church, we found that people wanted and even needed a purpose. It helped them to realize their potential. The

94

human body is the perfect example. Every part of the body has a purpose, and in life, there is power in purpose.

In a relationship, there is also power in purpose. Think about it – relationships help us to define and develop our true-identity. That's the most important part of being in a relationship. As a relationship progresses, we are constantly defining and developing ourselves. Relationships help us to learn to say "yes" and to say "no". Relationships teach us how to love and care, and how to accept love and care. The main idea is that all relationships serve a purpose. What is your purpose in a relationship? Ever really thought about it? Why are we in each others lives? A healthy relationship is going to be fair and balanced which will result in personal growth. We all want to be happy in our relationships. We want to feel love, happiness, contentment and appreciation. But at the same time, the purpose of a relationship is for us to show love, to show appreciation, and to make others feel happy and content.

My father's last station in the military was Keesler Air Force Base in Biloxi, Mississippi. I recently read a story that happened many years ago on a bridge not too far from Biloxi. A young lady was at the end of her ropes. She had experienced several traumatic events and decided to end her life. She drove her car out on a bridge that spanned the Mississippi River. She parked her car on the side of the bridge, got out and walked over to the rail. As she peered down in to the murky waters of the Mississippi River, she thought about her struggles and how she had lost her purpose in life. She didn't see any reason to keep living, so she climbed up on the railing and flung herself off. Unbeknownst to her, there was a man fishing from the bank who had just witnessed everything. He saw her park her car and walk over to the edge. He saw her slowly climb up on the railing and peer down in to the waters of the river. He saw her step off the rail and plunge toward the water. The woman's body hit the water with a terrible thud, and she began to sink to the bottom of the river. At about the same time, the man on the banks peeled off his shoes and dove in after her. He was able to get about 20 feet out in to the river when he realized he had forgotten one thing: He didn't know how to swim! The man started to flail about and struggle against the water. He quickly realized that he wasn't going to be able to save her or himself for that matter. Two people were drowning in the Mississippi River.

As the woman continued to sink toward the bottom of the river, she heard the splash and the commotion of the man now in the water. Something told her that he was in trouble and was drowning, so she stopped her descent and swam to the surface. She swam over to the drowning man and pulled him to the bank. The man and the woman laid there breathless just looking at one another. A passerby stopped and called 9/11, and an ambulance soon arrived to take them both to a local hospital. What's so interesting about the story is that a reporter wrote the following day about the incident. He said, "it wasn't the man who saved the woman's life – it was purpose that saved her life". We all need purpose in life. Purpose is like the fuel in an automobile engine. Without purpose, the engine of our soul begins to corrode, and in time it will shut down. That's why it's so important for us to continually be searching for purpose in our lives.

I have been counseling a disabled veteran for the last six months. Michael was deployed to Iraq in 2005, and halfway through the deployment, he was shot in the back. The bullet lodged near his spine. Michael said that as soon as he was shot, he knew something was wrong with his body. He was paralyzed from the waist down, and today is confined to a wheelchair. Several weeks ago, he said, "Mark, I don't feel

I have a purpose. I just don't think there is much I can do". I said, "ok then, quit thinking so much and start doing". To fulfill our purpose, we must do more than just think about it. Fulfilling your purpose requires "doing", and "believing". You may say, "well Mark, he's in a wheelchair – there's only so much he can do". The wheelchair, or the disability, is not the barrier in fulfilling potential. The main barrier in fulfilling your potential comes through the mind. It's in the believing. The most basic part of fulfilling your potential begins with relationships. God has placed you here to be involved in relationships, not only with Him, but also with others. That's why the Scripture says in Mark 12:30-31, "And you shall love the Lord your God with all your heart, with all your soul, with all your mind, and with all your strength. This is the first commandment. And the second, like it, is this: 'You shall love your neighbor as yourself.' There is no other commandment greater than these". That is your primary purpose in life – to be involved with others and to allow others to be involved with you. The key word being "love". You have a purpose, and God has given you the potential to fulfill that purpose. Your purpose will always begin with relationship.

Remember Chris my lawyer friend? His purpose is to be an attorney. He is great at it, and he loves what he's doing. My purpose wasn't to be an attorney. Although I think I would enjoy practicing law, it's not where my passion lies. Also, the arrows in my life just didn't point in that direction. I enjoy meeting people where they are in life and trying to help them move forward. I love being able to help people overcome problems. I enjoy ministry, but I really enjoy working with people one on one. Whose purpose has the most importance? Mine or his? Neither – God has created us to complete our mission – Chris has his purpose and I have mine. One mission is just as important as the next mission. I get frustrated sometimes with how people treat medical doctors or even pastors for that matter. Sometimes we tend to place people on a pedestal. We think that certainly their calling must be much higher and more important than ours. That is simply not the case. God has given you the potential to fulfill a purpose, and your purpose is just as important as anyone else.

One of my favorite jokes is about a man who arrived at the gates of heaven one day. St. Peter asked the man to give him one good reason why he should be allowed in to heaven. The man stands there scratching his head and thinking for a few minutes when finally, St. Peter said, "did you ever witness to people about me while you were living on earth?" "No, sir", replied the man. He continued to scratch his head trying to think of something when St. Peter said, "did you ever clothe the poor or feed the homeless while you were alive on earth?" "No, sir", came the reply. "Did you ever attend church or a small group when you were alive on earth?" Again the man replies, "No, sir". "Well what have you ever done on earth to get in to heaven, man?" St. Peter asked. "St. Peter, I was coming out of Wal-Mart when I saw four really big bikers picking on this little old lady. They had her surrounded, and one had her purse above her head. She was trying her best to jump up in the air and get it, but he wouldn't give it to her". St. Peter says, "Really? And what did you do?" "Well, sir, you know me. I went in to action. I went over to those bikers, and I hit the biggest one up side the head. I then pushed the one holding the purse up against the car and grabbed the purse away from him". "Wow", replied St. Peter, "when did all this happen?" The man looks at his watch and says, "about 15 seconds ago".

That's probably not the purpose that you are wanting to fulfill, especially with a similar result, but you do have a purpose. Do you remember the story of King David? Before he became a king, he was a sheep herder. One day his father tells him to take some refreshments out to his brothers who are serving on the front lines. I am sure David would have rather been on the battlefield with his brothers, but his duty was tending the sheep. So David went out to the battlefield to find the Israelite army cowering in fear from a huge problem called "Goliath". Goliath was nine feet tall, and he had challenged the Israelites. The problem was that no one was about to take him up on his challenge. Well, not until the young David came along. You probably remember the story well. David goes out on the battlefield with a slingshot and ends up killing Goliath. While all the Israelite warriors saw Goliath as a problem, David saw him as an opportunity.

David goes on to be a general and then a king. It seems like David had it going on in life. The Scripture says he was a man after God's own heart. But do you know what? David had problems throughout his life. It was one after another. David became a general but then had to flee because King Saul wanted to kill him. Later, David returned and became king. End of the story, right? Not quite! David continued to have problems. Remember he saw Bathsheba from a rooftop, and he starts thinking about her. He goes to his room and gives her a call. He says, "Hey Bathsheba, how would you like to go with me?" "Bathsheba replies, "Go where?" And David says, "you know, go together". Bathsheba says, "well David, I haven't seen you in a while". And David replies, "That's ok, I still look the same". Ok, maybe it didn't go quite like that, but it helps me emotionally to think that maybe it did.

What really happened was David had an affair with Bathsheba while her husband, Uriah, was fighting on the front lines. Bathsheba got pregnant, so to cover up her pregnancy, he sent for Bathsheba's husband to come home from fighting. David was hoping that Bathsheba and Uriah would have sex, and then the pregnancy could be explained. But Uriah refused to sleep with his wife while his men were fighting. So what did David do? He had Uriah sent back to the battlefield and placed on the front lines. If being on the front lines wasn't enough, King David ordered Uriah's men to abandon him during the heaviest of fighting. Uriah was killed and David married Bathsheba. Wow! Now remember, David was a man after God's own heart.

As a therapist, I see a lot of people who just can't seem to get over their past. I often hear, "Mark, I can't go here because I've been there", or "I can't do this because I have done that". To move toward your purpose, you must get over your past. You can't undo your past, but you can learn from it. I have thought many times in my past, "if David can do what he did, and still be a man after God's own heart, maybe I am not so bad after all". What the Scripture is telling me here is that God looks at the heart – not your past. And the truth is that finding your purpose will always require overcoming your past. God is not focused on your past – He is focused on your heart.

In counseling, the key to overcoming problems is always one of two things: It's either forgiving yourself or forgiving others. David still dealt with the consequences of his past as we all do, but David was able to focus on the here and now and know that God had forgiven him. When I begin therapy with a client, I always ask about forgiveness. In other words, is there anyone in your past that you have not forgiven? And then second, are there any instances in life where you may have not forgiven yourself? If we haven't been able to forgive ourselves or others, then it means we are "stuck" in the past. If we are stuck in the past, we cannot move forward in to the future.

The life of King David can teach us several lessons about purpose today. *First, it's all about your heart.* God doesn't consult your past – He consults your heart. *Second, God has equipped you to do something special.* Quit thinking about what you can't do and think about what God can do through you. God has a plan for your life, and the only thing that can come between His plan and your purpose is YOU. *Third, it is better to fear God than to fear your problem.* Goliath was nine feet tall, but David won the battle because he feared God. I am reminded that the beginning of true wisdom is a fear in God. *Fourth, David's success wasn't David's at all – it was God's.* David continually fell short throughout life. But he got right back up and kept going. David realized he was a work in progress. And *fifth, past sin can bring terrible consequences, but you can be forgiven.* We do face the consequences of our decisions, and the sum of all our decisions have brought us to where we are today. However, the decisions we make today will take us to where we will go tomorrow. And do you know what? It's never too late to start making good decisions.

The Power of Hope

As a Special Operations chaplain, I have seen very few atheists in combat. I have served with some of the toughest men in the world, but it's amazing how extreme danger can change your belief in a Higher Being. I remember a twenty-seven-year-old man who had a terrible childhood. His father had been an alcoholic and had physically abused him as a child. When the young man was 18 years old, he joined the military and volunteered for Special Operations. He told me that he did it just to see if he could make it. He was one of the more quieter ones in the unit, and it was well known with his friends that he didn't believe in God. I asked him one day why he didn't believe in God, and he said, "well chaplain, if there was a God, why would He allow such suffering in the world?". Sometime in 2006, this young man was deployed to Iraq. He was a part of a Special Operations recovery group and took part in several missions where he wondered if he would survive. Once he returned home, he came to my office to talk about "God". We spent several weeks getting together and discussing life and God. He would say, "Chaplain, I certainly believe there is a God now but I don't know what I think about Him". He wrestled with the idea "of God" for some time. But finally, after seeing death up close and realizing how fragile life really was, he placed his faith in God as his Comforter. He continued to deploy on a regular basis, and his relationship with God continued to grow. After almost ten years in the military, he ended up sensing a call to ministry. He was discharged from the service and later became a minister at a church in Montana.

The men in Special Operations might not have been the most ardent church-goers, but most believe in a higher being. One thing that combat teaches is that life is fleeting – it is here now and can be gone the next second. In combat, you see the worst of humankind. You see people trying to kill each other, and you see what no human being should ever have to see. But you also sense the good in humankind. You see young men and young women who left their homes to serve their country. They are serving because they believe in something greater than themselves. They believe in what America stands for, and they believe in each other.

Combat is a terrible experience, but at the same time, it teaches you what's really important in life.

As I reached my twenties, I had a lot of doubts in life. I didn't really know what I believed about God, or even if there was a God for that matter. Twenty something year old guys in the military tend to believe they are invincible. The military is excellent about breaking you down, and then building you up as a team. There's a lot of attitude and testosterone in a Combat Arms unit. As a nineteen year old, I never thought about death or dying. I was young and full of life, and anyway, how could the world keep going without me in it? Several experiences over the next year would help me to change my viewpoint about life and about death. When I was twenty years old, I was on a double date. We ended up going to a local Waffle House one night for a late supper. As we began looking at our menus, I noticed two young men across the restaurant who were flicking toothpicks across the tables. On several occasions, the toothpick would land in a middle-aged lady's hair sitting two booths down. The lady was there with her husband who looked to be in his mid-forties. The two young men continued to flick toothpicks, and finally after a few minutes, the husband got up and went over to their table.

The conversation became heated, and finally the two young men got up and left. The husband went back and sat down at his booth to finish his meal. About fifteen minutes later, the two men walked back in to the restaurant, and one pulled out a gun. He shot the middle-aged man in the back of the head, and then calmly turned and shot the telephone off the wall. The sound of the gun blast was both confusing and frightening. It was like I sensed the gun fire more than I heard it, and as soon as I sensed it, I was pushing my date under the table. I thought the shooter might begin shooting bystanders in the restaurant. What was so odd was the two men had pulled their car right up to the front door when they arrived the second time. As soon as the second shot was fired, they both turned around and walked back to their car and left. It was like a nightmare, and the moments after seemed like an eternity. My buddy and I ran over to the husband and immediately saw that he was dead. His wife was just sitting across from him staring at the top of his head. I never will forget the look on her face.

Within minutes, police were at the scene. Crime tape was put up all around the Waffle House, and everyone who had witnessed the crime were ordered to stay put for questioning. We gave the police officers a description of the men and of their car, and finally after about three hours, we were released to leave. I never will forget thinking how fast life could end. One second, the man was eating his meal, and the very next second he was dead. It really made me begin to think over the next few weeks. I wouldn't say that I automatically started thinking about the God of the Bible. But I did start thinking about life – and how delicate and fragile life really is. I also started thinking about hope, and the power hope has in life.

God allows us to experience life, and it always comes down to whether we just live through or actually learn from the experience. I look back over my life, and I see where God allowed certain experiences in life that built upon a past experience. About a year after the Waffle House tragedy, I lost a close friend in an accident. Craig was full of life and was always the life of the party. He was a big guy, and I never thought that anything could hurt him. When he was killed, I remember looking down at his lifeless body and thinking it was all some kind of joke. It couldn't be happening, but it was. Over the next several months, I continued thinking about life in general and how each one of us is literally an action or a choice away from death. Death is a cold hard fact, and we will all experience it, but what if there is more to death? What if death is just the closing of one chapter and the opening of another? Our hope is to have a better life, a better living, and better relationships, but the foundation of hope boils down to wishing for a better tomorrow both physically and eternally. When we truly comprehend the finality of death and the power of hope, we begin to see the potential of life. While many things may catch our eye, we learn what truly catches our heart.

Today we have a home in Helen, Georgia, but before we ever purchased the home, I enjoyed riding my motorcycle around the area. One day I was riding my motorcycle around the area enjoying Spring time weather and the winding roads. I pulled in to a local gas station to fill up and while I was at the gas pumps, another rider came riding up to the pumps. He was a big guy with hair down to the middle of his back and tied in a ponytail. He was riding a beautiful Harley Davidson, and he was decked out with leather and riding boots. He could have easily been mistaken for an outlaw motorcycle gang member. After filling my tank, I said, "nice bike, man", and we started to talk. Now you take two guys on motorcycles at a gas station, they are much more likely to talk about bikes than anything else.

He introduced himself as Ricky, and said he was originally from New England. Ricky had moved down to the Athens, Georgia area several years before and enjoyed riding his motorcycle up in to the North Georgia mountains every chance he got. Ricky asked me what I did for a living, and I told him that I was a minister. Ricky said, "you don't look much like a preacher to me". I didn't know whether to take that as a compliment or an insult. Ricky started telling me about his past. Come to find out, Ricky had served ten years in prison on drug charges and had only been released from prison three years before. He currently worked in the Athens area as a motorcycle mechanic and had been married and divorced several times. In all essence, Ricky was starting over in life. We talked for a few minutes about life, and then Ricky just out of the blue said, "I don't believe in God." Ricky proceeded to give me several reasons why he didn't believe.

After about ten more minutes of conversation, I said, "Ricky, here's the deal – you and I are different. I can give you the reasons why I believe there is a God, but I don't think you would ever listen to me. You've already got your mind made up. You have given God a verdict in your own heart, and I don't think you are willing to overturn it. Let me tell you this before we leave though. You go around that curve up the road and you wipe out on your bike – if there is no God, you are fine. It's a positive for you. I mean, you will never know it. But…if there is a

God, and you go around the curve and wipe out – it's going to be a negative for you because the Scripture says that we are all held accountable for our actions and what we believe". Ricky stared blankly at me. I went on, "now take me on the other hand – if I go around the curve and wipe out and there is no God – it's a positive for me because I will never know the difference. But if there is a God, it's also a positive because I chose to believe in Him. So Ricky, you live life with a positive and a negative, but I live life with a positive and a positive. See, I've got my bases covered". Ricky looked at me like I was crazy, got on his bike and drove off.

You know what happened? I pulled in behind him and started following him down the road. We got about five miles down the road and were passing a church in Sautee, Georgia called Nacoochee United Methodist Church. He puts his blinker on and points at the church. I follow him to the rear of the church, and we park our bikes. Ricky looked at me and said, "let me get your cell phone, dude, I might want to talk to you some more". We sat there and talked for almost three hours. Ricky called me several days later and wanted to meet one night. We met for dinner that evening and talked about God and life, and also about hope. Ricky gave his life to Christ that evening. Ricky told me that his life was full of negative experiences, and it was time to make a positive change. Ricky started attending church, and before long, he was involved in prison ministry. Today, Ricky is in prison ministry and has led hundreds of people to Christ. Oh, he still has long hair and a mustache and beard, and he still has tattoos all over his arms. But Ricky loves God – and he has since told me that he never thought he could be so happy and content in life. It's amazing how life works. God has a plan for Ricky, and while Ricky was serving those ten years in prison, God was preparing him. God was allowing him those experiences, as bad as they were, so that someday He could do something extraordinary in Ricky's life. And the same is true for you. God is using events, experiences, hardships, and struggles to bring you to a point of service. A place where your passion meets Kingdom work.

Let me tell you another very interesting part of the story. People say God doesn't have a sense of humor. Remember Nacoochee United Methodist Church? Several years later, I was called to be the senior pastor at the church and we moved to the area. Coincidence? Maybe and maybe not. The Bible says that "All things work for the good for those who love the Lord". That means that when you hold to your faith and continue serving God, things will somehow work out for the good.

The situation may look bleak to you and it may seem impossible. But with God, all things are possible.

I meet with people every week that cannot imagine how their current situation could ever turn out good. But it's all up to you and the hope that you cling to in life. I imagine that was the case for Hannah. Hannah's story is found in 1 Samuel and is a story of hope. Hannah was married to Elkanah, and her greatest hope was for a child. See, Hannah had wanted a child for years, but she had never been able to get pregnant. She had been ridiculed and provoked to the point to where she was desperate. So in a state of desperation, Hannah prays to God, and tells God that if He will bless her with a child, she will give that child back to Him. Hannah knew what she wanted, but she also knew how what she wanted could bless God. Does that make sense? In other words, Hannah was willing to pray for a blessing, but in turn, she was willing to give that blessing back to God.

Hannah was persistent, and she never gave up. Now listen to me because this is very important. God wants us to share our hopes and desires with Him. But in return, we should ask ourselves, "how am I willing to share my hope and desires if they come true?" Hannah wished for a child, but at the same time, Hannah lived in a day and age where she knew the Kingdom could use a man sold out to God, and she was willing to give her child back to God. Hope is very powerful especially when it's in tune with the needs of the Kingdom. Say you hope for a nice house – how can you use that house to bless God? Or maybe you are hoping to get a raise – how can you use that extra money to bless the Kingdom? Or maybe you want a nice retirement – how can you use that retirement to glorify God? Blessing and glorifying God comes through helping others. Again, it all boils down to relationship.

I knew a sixty-one year old man in Lexington, Kentucky who was homeless. His wife had passed away years before, and he didn't have any family. He had been homeless for about four years and stayed most nights at the Salvation Army Homeless Shelter on Main Street. For years, he had hoped and prayed for a home of his own. He would say, "I just hope I can own a home again one day before I die". At the time, I was working at the homeless shelter as a counselor. One day, he came rushing in to my office to tell me that he had found a job. He was going to start working at a local restaurant. He said, "it's only part-time but it's a start". He kept hoping, and he kept praying. Before long, he was working full time in the restaurant and doing an excellent job. By that time, he had rented a very small one bedroom apartment, but I continued to see him on a weekly basis. One day he told me, "Mark, you know what I would do if I owned a home?". He continued without even pausing for me to answer, "I would use the extra rooms to help people get off the street – that's what I would do". Within a year, he was working as an assistant manager in the restaurant and soon after he bought a house. His dream had come true. As soon as he moved in, he called me at the shelter and said, "Mark, remember when I told you I would move homeless people in? – well, do you have any one that needs a room?" We started sending homeless families to his home where he would provide them a room. His rooms stayed full. It wasn't long until he had two homes, and he was continuing to help people get off the streets. The last I heard, he had three homes and continues to help homeless people. Pretty good for a guy that dreamed of one day owning a home. I believe that's how God wants us to be when it comes to hope. It's ok to hope and to ask for what you want, but at the same time, what are you willing to do with your blessings? Hope is powerful in our lives. It keeps us going day after day. It helps us to try and be better than what we are. And it pushes it to greater limits in life.

The greatest hope is that death will not be the end but only the beginning. 1 Peter 1:3-6 says, "Praise be to the God and Father of our Lord Jesus Christ! In His great mercy He has given us new birth into a living hope through the resurrection of Jesus Christ from the dead, and into an inheritance that can never perish, spoil, or fade. This inheritance is kept in heaven for you, who through faith are shielded by God's power until the coming of the salvation that is ready to be revealed in the last time. In all this you greatly rejoice, though now for a little while you may have had to suffer grief in all kinds of trials". Hope is what keeps us going when we don't feel like going any further. Think about when you were in high school or college – you didn't want to get up and go to class. It was hope that got you up, and got you to class. Maybe you were hoping for the weekend to come, or maybe it was the summer. Or maybe you got up and went to class because you were hoping that one day you would be out of school and wanting to find a job. Hope gets you up each day, and it's hope that pushes you forward.

When I was in the Air Force, I had the opportunity to get certified in Applied Suicide Intervention Training (ASIST). At the time, the military was certifying as many people as possible because the suicide rate was at an all-time high and climbing higher each year. The military has been a strictly volunteer organization for several decades and hasn't had a draft in place since Vietnam. Young men and women visit the military recruiter full of hope and expectation. I remember taking the ASVAB entry test and then going to the Military Entrance Processing Station (MEPS) to complete a physical and learn what I was qualified to do in the military. If you passed the ASVAB and the physical portion, you were then placed on a computer to "contract". All the jobs that you were qualified to do were shown and you were given "ship dates", or dates to depart for Basic Training. You then went home to pass by time until your ship date arrived.

It was exciting times to say the least. I remember arriving for basic training that first day. I was excited yet nervous. I was full of hope for whatever was ahead. I would say it's normal for each person joining the military to have the same feelings. Feeling of hope, anxiety, and even nervousness is very common. So if life is so good in the military, why is the suicide rate so high? Good question! Young men and women go to basic training with feelings of hope and anxiety, but then perhaps some bad things begin to happen. For some, they may not like the structured setting of basic training. Some men and women enter the service looking forward to deploying overseas only to find out that the deployment is not what they expected. I know many veterans who have served honorably. They served their country, and they gave it their all. But many return home with little hope. They come back to their bases or their hometowns, and life doesn't seem to be how they remember.

As a chaplain and counselor, we were trained to help young men and women identify the triggers leading to depression and post-traumatic stress. We try to help identify those young men and women who may be feeling hopeless and helpless. We also had the task of helping them rebuild hope in their lives. Sometimes it's difficult for us to understand the "process" of life. In other words, it's like all of our experiences are pieces to a puzzle. We are constantly in the process of completing a puzzle throughout our lives, and on the day we die, we will have put together a picture. Some of us will have a wonderful picture put together at the end of life. It's up to us to take the experiences of our lives, and piece them together to create a picture. Depression creeps in when we get to a place in life where we don't understand how the pieces to our puzzle are fitting together. We lose sight of who we thought we were or who we think we should be, and it throws our lives off kilter.

Hope is powerful. It tells us that there is always a tomorrow. For the Christian, hope tells us that there is life after death. And when we tie our hope in with our faith, we are unstoppable. There is no wall that you cannot climb and no barrier that you cannot overcome. I read the story of a farmer who lived on a ranch in central Texas back during the depression. The ranch had been in his family for over 100 years. Times were tough, and the farmer's family barely had enough food to survive. No matter how hard he worked, he couldn't save enough money each month to make his mortgage payment. Finally, the banker came out to the farmer's ranch one day and gave him the impending news. The banker told him that he would need to be caught up on his payments within the next three months or the bank would foreclose on the property. The farmer worked from daylight to dark but still couldn't make enough to pay the month's mortgage, so he sank deeper and deeper in to debt.

A couple of weeks before the bank was to foreclose, the farmer sank to his knees in desperation. He said, "God, if it's not your will for me to have this farm, I will gladly move away and start all over. But Lord, this has been in my family for 100 years. If there is any way I can keep it, I will promise You to use it to help others". A couple of days before the bank was to take possession, a young man showed up one morning at the ranch. He said, "Sir, do you mind if I do some prodding around on your land. I want to check the area out and see what's around here"? The man said, "Yea, go ahead- I'm about to lose it anyway". So the young man goes on his way. The next day, the farmer hears knock on his door. There stood the young man beaming from head to toe. He said, "Sir, I think you've got oil on your land". In the end, the man struck oil on his property before the bank foreclosed. He paid off the bank, and he went on to open an orphanage on the ranch. The story goes that not only did he open an orphanage, but he bought the bank that was to repossess his land. The rancher was willing to ask God for a blessing, but the farmer also knew how he could bless God with his blessings.

****

Hope and faith go hand in hand. For me, my mother is an example of faith and hope. I have three sisters, and she calls each one of us at least a few times each week. She just wants to check on us and know that we are ok. When we are traveling to see my parents, she will normally stay up until we get there. My parents didn't always get along. I mean, they argued just like other parents. My dad retired out of the Air Force when he was 42 years old. Now dad was prone to drink "a few" beers. He bought a local gas station in Reeltown, and then bought a camper. He backed the camper up to the back of the store, and it became "nap" central. Every day around noon, dad would disappear around back to get his "nap".

Back during that time, dad got really interested in the Oprah Winfrey Show. I used to tease him about having a crush on her. I always got out of the way when Oprah came on because to get in dad's way could have some serious consequences. We used to tease him about the three most dangerous things in life. 1. To be tied to the tracks as a steaming locomotive was coming. 2. To get kicked in the head by a wild mule. 3. To get in dad's way when Oprah came on. I would probably say the third would be the most dangerous. Dad would run over you. Dad may have had his naps and watched Oprah every day, but he worked really hard around the store. He would open the store each morning at 5:30am, and then close the store each night at 8:00pm. I don't know how he held out. But like he always says, "I'm a worker!". The thing about dad is his ingenuity. He always said that "skill and ingenuity always wins out over luck and superstition". Dad has always been able to look at a problem and figure out a fix for it. He has invented some really neat gadgets in his time. Back in the 80's, dad took a level and attached a small laser beam to the top of it. He could level the wall, and then shoot the beam across the room to get an exact measurement. He showed me his invention one day, and I said, "Dad, you need to send this in – I bet you could make some money with this contraption". About fifteen years later, I noticed local hardware stores started selling something very similar. See, Dad? You could have gotten rich if you had sent it in.

My mom has a prayer closet, and she spent a lot of nights praying for dad – and for me too. Mom says she almost gave up praying for him, and I am sure they talked about divorce a few times. But she hung in there. Mom always hoped that dad would quit drinking, and she wanted him to take part in church. Mom prayed for years, and those years turned in to decades. But in 1988, my dad "saw the light". He straightened his life out and quit smoking and drinking. He started attending church, and later was ordained a deacon. I used to think I had it pretty rough, but I wouldn't take anything for those days at the store. I made two dollars an hour, but I probably ate ten dollars an hour in groceries. We never wanted for anything growing up, and mom and dad were great parents. Today, they may fuss sometimes, but mostly they sit around watching Fox News and enjoying each other. Mom's dream came true. She has dad all to herself every day. Oh, and dad's dream came true as well. Well, kinda. The good thing is that he doesn't have to slip around the back of the store to the old camper for his nap. He takes his nap in his recliner at home each day. The bad news is The Oprah Winfrey Show went off the air, so now dad sits around and watches Fox News. Hope is what keeps the engine of our soul running.

The Power of Temptation

Ever heard of a Liger? A liger is a cross between a lion and a tiger. Believe it or not, there are people around the world who illegally purchase such animals for display in their homes. I know – weird! One couple lived in the Pacific Northwest. They were intrigued by the liger and decided to purchase one. So they prepared a cage in their carport and ordered the cat. They loved having the liger in their carport, and when friends would come over, they would take them in to the carport and proudly display their prize. The liger was beautiful and even seemed somewhat tamed behind the bars of the cage. One day, some friends came to visit who had a ten-year-old daughter. The couple quickly took them out to the carport to show them their pet. They stood around the cage marveling at the beauty of the cat. After the adults went back in to the house, the ten-year-old daughter stood in the carport looking at the cat. It looked so friendly, so she decided to pet it. She reached her arm in to the cage and began gently stroking the top of the cat's head. At first, everything was ok. The liger seemed to be enjoying the girl's attention when all of a sudden, the cat's entire countenance changed. Before she could react, the liger grabbed the young girl by her shoulder and started trying to pull her in the cage. The more the girl struggled, the firmer the cat's hold. The girl was shrieking in terror when her parents came running in to the carport. The father grabbed a broom handle and started hitting the cat over the head to no avail. Finally, the cat's owner ran inside and retrieved his pistol. It took a bullet to the cat's head before it would let go but not before it had caused terrible scars to the shoulder and arm of the young girl.

Temptation is like that liger. It's can look good from a distance, but up close it's dangerous. And when you take part in it, it can create scars that will last for the rest of your life. I remember one evening a friend coming to the barracks and asking me if I wanted to go to Live Oak, Florida. It was 1988, and I was stationed in Jacksonville. He said, "Mark, I've got a case of beer man – let's go!". It was a Saturday, and life in the barracks could be very boring. I told him I wasn't going to go because I had to be on duty the next day, but he kept on. There was like a second sense telling me not to go, but I ignored it, and I agreed to go. We drove out to Live Oak and spent the evening drinking beer. When it was time to go back to Jacksonville, my friend told me that he was in no condition to drive. My second mistake of the evening was volunteering to drive back. I ended up running off the road in Baldwin, Florida and getting arrested for Driving Under the Influence.

As I mentioned earlier, every action has a consequence. Not only was I arrested and placed in the Duval County Jail, but I stayed in jail until the following Monday morning. I was supposed to be at the base on Sunday morning, and when I didn't show, I was reported as Absent Without Leave (AWOL). Not only were there consequences in Duval County, but I was also sent to "Captain's Mass" and placed on restriction for 30 days on base. It was like double jeopardy. That split second decision to ride to Live Oak with my friend had many consequences over the coming years. I had just been promoted to E-5, but I lost the promotion. I lost my license for six months and lost all base driving privileges for one year. I had to buy a bicycle to get around on base, and believe me, I wore the tires off it the next year. Taking part in temptation will always create scarring in one way or another. Sometimes you can't see the scars from a distance, but when you get close, the scars are evident. It reminds me of an incident that happened in Tallassee, Alabama back in the 1980's.

Rumor was that a man had gone in to the local Hardee's to get something to eat late one night. Hardee's had already closed for the night, so the man began to bang on the door shouting for someone to make him a hamburger. The man became very angry when no one would open the door, so he went to his truck and pulled out an ax and commenced to chopping the telephone pole down. Apparently, the local police thwarted his plan but not before he had permanently damaged the pole with ax marks. The pole remained in front of Hardee's for years and still served a purpose, but the ax marks were a testament to it's past. And we are the same. We may look good on the outside, but most of us have endured experiences in life that have created scars. You may not see our scars from a distance, but when you get close they become more evident. Listen, scars are not a bad thing. Matter of fact, those scars are permanent markers and are a part of who we are. They help direct and guide us in finding our potential and fulfilling our purpose. When we are willing to use them, they become a powerful source for us to use in helping others.

Tempt in the Greek language is "poradzo". It's meaning is to be enticed into sin or to have your faith tested. The thing about temptation is that it is different for each individual. Temptation is anything that, by you taking part in it, takes your eyes off God. It's always seems better, quicker, and easier but in the end it is always more difficult and usually painful. From premarital sex, to lust, to lying, to making yourself look better in front of others – it always looks, sounds, and feels good on the surface. But beneath it's surface, the reward is always short term with long term consequences. For one person, temptation may be looking at someone in a sexual nature. For another person, it may be a desire to make themselves look bigger and better in the eyes of others. For another person, temptation can come by way of just wanting stuff. Temptation can even come through how and what you think about yourself. See, Satan knows your weakness and he attacks us where we are weak. But temptation is not the sin. Taking part in the temptation and carrying it to the next level is the sin that creates scars.

Only one person ever completely overcame temptation and never sinned, and that was Jesus Christ. We can get an idea how to overcome temptation by studying the life of Jesus. Jesus did three things while He was being tempted. He prayed and meditated, He fasted, and He quoted

Scripture. The key to overcoming temptation in our lives is through prayer, fasting and knowing or memorizing Scripture. Prayer is talking to God while reading and knowing Scripture is God talking to you. And fasting is curbing the desires of our flesh. Several years ago I heard a very interesting sermon on fasting. The speaker said that fasting is important because temptation is all about our bodies giving in to our desires where fasting is all about our desires giving in to our bodies (the temple of God). The key to potential is realizing that even if you have fallen in to temptation, God is not finished with you. God doesn't take away your potential when we fall short. He continues throughout our lives to give us opportunities to reach our potential and fulfill His purpose. When it comes to understanding how temptation works in our lives, it is important to understand the formers of the universe.

God is the *former* of potential. As we talked about earlier, it is God who formed your potential. He has placed within you a seed of greatness and when the right conditions are met, your potential will result in God's purpose being fulfilled. Remember your potential is related to God's potential because He is at work in and through you. But at the same time, it is Satan who wants to *deform* your potential. He wants to take that which is good and make it in to something which is bad. In other words, when God creates your potential, Satan wants to destroy it. Satan wants to destroy your potential, and he does it through temptation. Ever wanted to do something and then think to yourself, "I can't do that. I am not good enough or I'm just not capable?". That's Satan whispering the same lie that he whispered to Eve thousands of years ago. I have always told our kids, "God has given you the ability to lead people toward God and toward good, and you have the ability to lead people away from God and toward bad – the decision is completely yours". And it is completely yours also. God has given you the free will to make that decision, but remember, that decision will literally affect the lives of many more people than just your own.

God is the former, and Satan is the deformer of potential. But do you now what? Jesus is the _transformer_ of potential. That which God made is good, but Satan comes along and tries to make it bad. Jesus came to earth to transform the bad back in to good. Does that make sense? We seek transformation through Christ from the deformation by Satan. Satan is intend on deforming anything that is good in your life, and when we allow him, he will literally destroy our lives. So if God is the God of the universe, why does he give Satan so much latitude here on earth? Why does God even allow us to be tempted? I mean, wouldn't life be much easier if God never allowed us to be tempted? As I mentioned in the beginning of the book, I am not an expert on God or the Bible, but I know what I believe. In God's infinite wisdom, He loves you enough to give you a choice. He gives you options throughout life. If He is the author of good, then something or someone else must be the author of bad. It goes back to the law of opposites. Let me try to answer the above questions with a story which will help you understand why God allows temptation.

As the Union Pacific Railroad was being constructed; an elaborate trestle bridge was built across a large canyon in the West. Wanting to test the bridge, the builder loaded a train with enough extra cars and equipment to double its normal payload. The train was then driven to the middle of the bridge, where it stayed an entire day. One of the workers approached the builder and said, "Sir, are you trying to break the bridge?". "No", said the builder, "I am trying to prove that the bridge won't break". In the same way, the temptations that Jesus faced were not allowed by God to see if Christ would sin, but to prove that He wouldn't sin. And even for you the same is true. God does allow you to be tempted each and every day. But God allows those temptations in life not so much to break you but to build you. When you make the right decision based on purpose, faith and belief, it opens up powerful

possibilities in your life.

Living and Learning

In private practice, I like to discuss the 4 Aspects of Life, or the 4 Parts of Life. We have the physical, the mental, the emotion, and the spiritual. When we have a physical problem, we go to see a medical doctor. When we have an emotional or mental problem, we may go to see a psychologist or a counselor. But so often when we have spiritual problems, we just sweep them under the rug and go on with life. We live our lives with hatred, envy, and pride. We are negative about ourselves and others, and sometimes we gossip too much. But if you mention the problem to us, we like to say, "hey, that's just who I am – God made me that way!". No, He didn't. If you imagine those four parts on a bar graph, each one must be even and consistent. In other words, we must work hard to stay physically healthy. I enjoy working out at the gym, and I like to hike. I want to watch my weight and try to eat a healthy diet. The same is true with the mental, emotional and spiritual. We stay mentally healthy by exercising our brain and by learning new things. We stay emotionally healthy through the relationships we keep in life. We love each other, and yes, we even love ourselves. We need to love and we need one anther's love. But what about the spiritual aspect?

We are spiritual beings. The fact that you can dream, plan and even hope is proof that there is a spiritual side. It's very important to be aware that you are a spiritual being. You are not just physical. You have yearnings and hope and even a conscience. God has placed within you a desire to do good and to love one another. Now I am not saying that you must go to church and sing in the choir every Sunday to practice your spirituality. But you do need to have faith and belief in a higher order – in a supreme being. We are connected to God, and when we are willing to draw close to Him, we realize and sense His proximity to us.

I have heard pastors say that you need to be in church every Sunday to spiritually grow. They would say that you must be doing "something in the church" in order to have a relationship with God. But personally, I don't believe that. I believe that we do need to be in relational living with other people who are like minded in their faith, but I believe that you must first and foremost be willing to seek and establish a relationship with God. And I believe God will direct you from there. You can find God in your house, or in your back yard. I have often found God in hospital rooms and nursing homes. I have pastored several great churches, and I am not speaking of any specific church, but there are churches that actually separate people from God. I know, I know – it's sounds hypocritical for me to say that. But it's true. I have been in churches that are much more focused on programs than they are on people. Many are more focused on money than they are on ministry. Some are focused more on power than they are on purpose. Over the last fifty years, many people have left the church and the faith because they equate Christians as being hypocritical and maybe judgmental. We have seen financial and sexual scandals that have rocked denominations. All this to say, we haven't always represented Jesus Christ and the true nature of faith.

Pastors often deal with "control" issues in the church. Some people have all the right intentions, but they come in to the church and want to control certain things. I mean let's face it, we all want to be happy and have our needs met. Maybe we want the music one way or the other. Or maybe the preacher isn't preaching to our liking. Sometimes we may get mad, and maybe create some tension in the church. Sometimes we may just quit attending all together. Whether we are a pastor or member, we cannot attend church with a personal agenda. If we come to church and get angry because the music isn't to "our liking", or if we don't like it because "someone sat in our seat", we are establishing our own agenda. In all essence, we replace Jesus with our own agenda, and thus begin to worship an image of ourselves and our desires.

I served at a homeless shelter in Lexington, Kentucky for two years. It was a wonderful experience. A middle-aged couple came to the shelter one Friday night. They only had the clothes they were wearing which was blue jeans and t-shirts. They had recently lost their home and had migrated to Lexington in search of employment and a new beginning. When they were checking in to the shelter, they asked about local churches and worship times. They woke up early on Sunday morning and walked over to a church not far from the shelter. They were excited to worship and to sense the presence of God. As they walked in to the church, an older gentleman approached them and asked if they needed help. They responded to him by saying that they were there to attend worship. The older man went on to inform them that they couldn't attend worship without "Sunday clothes". The couple turned around and walked out. I never will forget meeting with them the next day. The woman was crying and said, "I was so embarrassed that we didn't have anything better to wear". By the time they left my office, I was so angry that I called the pastor to inform him what had happened. My idea was that the pastor needed to know about this problem, so he could address it with the older gentleman. The pastor listened as I shared the story, and then responded that the church had a dress code and maybe we could find them "more appropriate clothes" if they wanted to come back. I said, "Preacher, I promise you, they don't want to come back!".

Over the next several weeks, the couple struggled with going to church in general. The husband told me that they "might just hang up" going to church. I could understand their feelings – they were hurt and embarrassed. But to me it was almost as if they were punishing God. I met with them for almost a month, and we talked about how church attendance isn't between "you and them". It's between "you and God". I'm sure that particular church had many positive things going on, but in that situation, they had given Jesus a bad name. The Church must try to pattern a Christ-like behavior. Would Jesus have turned the couple away from worship? Certainly not. So should you attend church? It all depends. Don't attend church just because it's called a "church". Many churches don't represent Jesus well because they are judgmental, prone to gossip, or maybe have a spirit of control. Church attendance is important for all believers, but it's also very important to find a church that is going to represent Jesus. Is the church all about programs or people - power or purpose - money or ministry?

We are called to a "Living Faith". A living faith demands that we live out our faith on a daily basis. People are either living for the moment or living by the moment. Most of us "live for the moment" when we are young. We just want to have fun, and we oftentimes don't think about the consequences of our actions. As we reach older adulthood, most of us go from living for the moment to living by the moment. In other words, we are not after the adventure and thrill of our youth. Living for the moment is doing whatever it takes to make "me" feel good. Our culture has geared us toward the idea that we should always be happy and our needs must be met. Living by the moment is different. Living by the moment implies that we not take each moment for granted, but we consider the moment and it's place in developing our potential and purpose. Every moment is important in life – and what we do with each moment counts.

Several years ago, I served a church in Commerce, Georgia. New Salem was one of the most giving churches that I have ever attended. The people would look for ways to reach out, and they loved each other. During my two years at the church, I never heard one negative word from a member about another member. New Salem had been burned to the ground in 1998 by a satanist. Basically, the guy traveled through Tennessee and Georgia setting churches on fire. When he decided to burn New Salem, he pulled around the back of the church and started the fire. As the church began to burn, the local fire department was called out. A young man named Loy Williams was one of the first firemen to arrive on the scene. As the flames grew higher, Loy and several firemen went inside the church to try and get the fire under control. The firemen were willing to do what it took to save the old church, but it wasn't to be. The roof collapsed on Loy and killed him. The church was completely burned to the ground, and the good people of New Salem were left wondering if they had a "next chapter" in ministry. The church had an insurance policy worth about $88,000, and the members realized that God would have to show up in a mighty way if they were ever to build a church on that amount.

The congregation began having worship services in a shed that stood beside the charred church, and they prayed. The church building that had burned was an old building, but the people of New Salem had never been so much worried about "the looks". The little shed served the purpose, and they were just happy to be able to come together. They had a physical location, and although the fire and death of Loy had been a traumatic and emotional time, they continued to love and support each other. Before long, God started moving. A youth group from Israel arrived to lay a foundation for a new church building. Scriptures were written in the foundation in dedication to God and the future of the church. People continued to show up and donate items. The men would work at the church site each day while the women made sandwiches for lunch. There was unity, and a sense of togetherness. The church building slowly began to take shape. One day, a roofer was traveling past the church and noticed the building almost finished but no shingles on the roof. He pulled in to the church and asked if they were in need of a roofer. It's amazing how God works, but that was the main need at that time. The roofer was finishing a large roofing project not far from the church, and said he would have some left over materials to begin the job.

In the end, the roofer had enough shingles and roofing material to finish the church.

The congregation was excited to have a new church building. They had built a beautiful 1.3 million dollar church building with little or no debt. A very interesting thing happened a few months later. A man pulled in to the church one day and asked if he could have a stump of wood off an old charred tree that stood beside the church. He cut a large piece of the wood and promised to return with a surprise. Several months later, the man brought a beautiful hand-carved piece of wood to the church. It was a carving of Jesus rising out of the flame and blowing a trumpet. The piece of wood sits in the foyer of the church to this day. It's a reminder that Jesus continues to rise out of the flames of life, and even when life appears hopeless, we can be victorious in our situation through Him.

Proverbs 3:5-6 says, "Trust in the Lord with all your heart and lean not on your own understanding; in all your ways submit to Him, and He will make your paths straight". I know God was at work through the prayers and efforts of the New Salem congregation. It wasn't so much that their prayers were more powerful than any other congregation, but I believe God answered their prayers because their hearts were right before God. They weren't in competition with other local churches, and they weren't trying to build the biggest or best program. They were excited to have a new building, but the building was just an ends to a means. In other words, it was just a place for the church to meet. They simply wanted to honor God and be together, and at the same time, share with others what God had been doing in their past. And through their effort, they witnessed God doing some amazing things.

Growing Older Happier

If you know anything about explosives, you know that C-4 is a common variety for a plastic explosive family known as Composition C. C-4 has a texture similar to molding clay and can be molded into any desired shape or form. What makes C-4 different is that it's very stable and the explosion can only be initiated by a combination of extreme heat and shock wave from a detonator. Our lives are very similar. We are shaped and formed by experiences and situations throughout life. We are the sum of all the decisions we have made throughout life. Our potential is like the detonator in the explosive. When we begin to reach our potential, we start seeing our lives change and new opportunities open around us. I don't know about you, but I want to "grow old happy". I don't want to one day look back on my life and wonder if I lived life to the best of my ability.

My dad is a great example. He probably didn't have the best childhood, and he grew up during the Great Depression. He served a tour in Vietnam in 1969, but if he has ever been depressed, no one could tell it. He's always happy, and he seldom complains. At least not to me. Dad seems happy for the day. He is excited to be up and about and to have the health to "feel good". In his mid-eighties now, his favorite hobby is touring the garden on his tractor. He calls it work. Mom says that every time she sees him outside, he has his hands in his pockets. But dad is happy. He's ok with where he is in life. He doesn't have anything to prove to anyone. Dad will go out to work in the yard, and each time he comes back in, he tells mom to "feel my back – I'm a worker!" I think he pours a cup of water down his back and then tries to impress mom because sometimes he's actually sweating a little bit.

Dad loves to go to church. No offense, dad, but I think his favorite part of church is getting to hug some of the young women's necks. My sister, Pam, has a friend named Michelle. Every time dad is around Michelle, he tells us how many times she hugged his neck. We were leaving church one day and dad says, "Mark, how many times did Michelle hug your neck?". I said, "None". Dad says with this sly smile, "she hugged my neck about five times". Mom's fine with it – she knows dad isn't looking for a date. He just enjoys being around people. Anytime a few people gather together, dad starts sharing stories from the past. All this to say, when I get dad's age, I want the same attitude about life. I want to be able to look back, and although there have been some hard times, I want to be able to focus on "what's ahead".

Dad doesn't expect more or less in life– he's just content. My parents have always been quick to help others. My mom fusses all the time because she gets calls from telemarketers asking for money. But the reason they keep calling her is because she will usually cave in and give them a few bucks. When someone calls the house, dad will usually give the phone to mom. He calls her "his mouthpiece". But mom loves people also. When we are sitting around the table at dinnertime, mom will constantly ask each one of us what we want. "Mark, get you some more cornbread". "Keller, eat the rest of those potatoes". "Heather, you want some more tea?" Now mom is 83 years old, and if someone's glass hits empty, she's up and moving around to get the tea. Mom loves to serve people, and she wants people to feel welcome in their home. It has been my mother that has given me a glimpse of the love that God has for His children.

I am learning that growing older happier is a mindset. But it also has to do with being able to laugh at yourself, and yes, at times laugh at others. It's like the old saying goes, "if you won't laugh at yourself - I will". Don't take life so serious. God placed you on earth to enjoy life. Life is what you determine it will be each and every morning. I speak with people every week who are depressed. For many of them, they have focused on past failures and mistakes, and they have lost sight of how those experiences can be used for a bright future. My job as a therapist is to help them learn from their past, and at the same time, to always look toward their future. "Growing old" is the most important journey we will ever take, and every single person alive is on the journey. We determine whether the journey is going to be a good one or a bad one. One of the most important aspects of the journey is realizing that someone is always watching you. In other words, you are setting the example for someone in your life.

When I served as the pastor at Nacoochee United Methodist Church, a man named Lee Hardy served on the Church Leadership Board. Lee was a few years older than me, and we became close friends very quickly. No matter what was going on, Lee could always get others to smile. At the time, Lee was dating a beautiful lady named Betty who started coming to church with him. Betty had been a principal and had recently retired. One day they came in to my office with a request – they wanted to get married during a worship service on a Sunday. I asked them when they wanted to get married, and they said "whenever you're ready". I just happened to be preaching a sermon series on commitment, so we scheduled a date for the wedding. Over the next several weeks, we didn't tell a soul. On the day of the wedding, I was closing the sermon on commitment to God and to one another, and said to the congregation, "Today, we have a personal example of commitment". At that time, the pianist started playing "Here Comes the Bride", and Betty started walking down the aisle. It caught every one by surprise, but by the end of the service, there wasn't too many dry eyes in the building. Both Betty and Lee were an inspiration to not only me, but to everyone in the church. After church, we had a celebration honoring the commitment that they had made to God and to one another.

I ended up leaving the church a few years later, but Lee and I stayed in touch. Several years later, Lee was diagnosed with cancer. He began to lose weight as he fought for his life. I wasn't able to see Lee often, but I noticed each time I saw him that he had lost a few more pounds. A few weeks before Lee died, he told me something I will never forget. He said, "Mark, I have always felt like God wanted me to set a good example for my children. Growing old and dying is no different. God still calls me to set an example, but now I am setting the example of how to die with faith and honor". I want them to learn from me how to die gracefully and in peace". I will never forget Lee's words because they live on in my heart.

We are called to set the example for others around us, and it's a very important responsibility. Someone is watching you today – the question is – what are they seeing? There are five things you can do to grow old happy. First, don't take yourself to seriously. As mentioned earlier, be willing to laugh at yourself. Make sure you have relationships in your life that create laughter. The greatest influence in life comes through relationships. We begin to pattern our lives through the company that we keep. Take addiction for example, a person seldom will kick the habit of addiction if they are continuing to hang around addicts. The same is true for happiness in life. Several months ago, I started working with a young man who was depressed. He has been through some terrible experiences in life, and it has had a major affect on him today. During our second meeting, we started talking about the importance of relationships in life. I asked him to identify some of the characteristics of "his" relationships.

I quickly noticed that he seldom spent time around people who were happy. Matter of fact, most of his time was spent alone. If we are going to be happy in life, we must surround ourselves with people who laugh and who are happy. Laughing helps us keep our troubles in proportion because it helps us to create a positive emotion in life.

Ever met anyone that liked to laugh at others but couldn't laugh at themselves? People who have a difficult time laughing at themselves tend to be perfectionists and often are the ones who are easily angered at themselves. What's so amazing about laughter is that statistics show that children laugh 200 times per day while adults only 26 times per day. If you want to grow old happy, learn to laugh at yourself. Don't take everything so serious especially your past. God will forgive – claim it and move on.

Second, don't get so focused on the failures from your past that you fail to see opportunities today. Focusing on the past does two things: First, it causes bitterness, and second, bitterness will lead to depression. Learn to look at your past experiences positively. I know, I know, sometimes it's hard to look at a failure as being positive. But you can make every experience a positive if you learn from it, and in turn, figure out a way to use it to help others. Experience, both good and bad, is the seasoning of life. Always remember, God will use what you learn from your past experiences to help you today, and also to prepare you for tomorrow.

Third, realize that you always have a future. People grow hopeless because they forget that there is always a better tomorrow. No matter who you are, a better tomorrow awaits you. You just have to see it and claim it. Faith is the link between hope and tomorrow. From our low points in life, we gain strength, and from our high points in life, we gain happiness. People who grow old happy learn to acknowledge the bad but never dwell on it. They learn to dwell on the good in life. Sometimes it feels as if the world is against us, but faith in God tells us that we always have a brighter tomorrow.

Fourth, stay physically, mentally, emotionally and spiritually fit. Take care of yourself. 1 Corinthians 6:19 says, "Do you not know that your bodies are temples of the Holy Spirit, who is in you, whom you have received from God? You are not your own..." God the Father created our bodies. God the Son redeemed them, and God the Holy Spirit indwells them. When you begin to treat your body with the same reverence you might treat a temple, I believe that it will open up blessings for you.

And fifth, know that there is a God and He loves you. We cannot understand the intricacies of life, but we realize that through faith we see not with our eyes what can only be seen with our hearts. I was talking to someone a few weeks ago who said they weren't a person of faith. But the fact is that everyone is a person of faith. God has given each person a certain level of faith. I would argue that we all have about the same level of faith. It's just that for many of us, our faith is spread out. In other words, we have faith in different things. Some of us choose to have faith in a Higher Being – God. I choose to have faith that Jesus Christ is the Son of God, and He died for my sins. Just because someone doesn't believe like I do doesn't mean they lack faith. I have a friend who doesn't have faith in God, but he has faith in himself – his wife – and even his job. Is he wrong about faith? No, he's not – he has faith. But he is wrong about where his faith belongs. Our faith belongs to God – because God is our Creator and our Sustainer. When we place our faith in God, and when we choose to live according to His Word, we begin to sense the love that He has for us. When our faith is in anything other than God – faith is still there – it's just not grounded to it's source.

Remember the analogy of the apple tree? When we are connected to our source, our faith will espouse who we are and what we are here to accomplish. The fact is that God loves you – He really does! Faith should always remind us of His love.

***

I look back over my life, and I see what I like to call spiritual markers. A spiritual marker is a place where God has shown up in your past. In the Book of Joshua, the Israelites would pile up stones as spiritual markers, Joshua 4:6-7 says, "that this may be a sign among you when your children ask in time to come, saying, 'What do these stones mean to you'" Then you shall answer them that the waters of the Jordan were cut off before the ark of the covenant of the Lord; when it crossed the Jordan, the waters of the Jordan were cut off. And these stones shall be for a memorial to the children of Israel forever." The Israelite's used the stones to mark the place where God had shown up in their life. It was a testament and a reminder not only to them but to their children as well.

Each one of us have spiritual markers in our life. As you look back over your past, God has shown up in mighty ways. Sometimes we acknowledge Him and see His work around us, and sometimes we get so busy with "life" that we fail to see Him at work. When I think about my own spiritual markers, I am reminded of my children's birth. As I saw them being born, I remember thinking that there was no way it could be a coincidence. There had to be "something" or "someone" behind the scenes. Life truly indeed is a miracle. The death of my friends and family members serve as a spiritual marker for me because I am reminded that we are only here for a short time, and then we all go to meet our Maker. I think about the day I became a Christian – that was a spiritual marker. God was doing something in and through me, and I could feel it. Spiritual markers remind us of the places where God has shown Himself in our past. You may say, "Mark, I don't think God has ever shown Himself to me". But hasn't he? When we look around us and think about creation and life in general, we are reminded of a higher order. God uses those questions and mysteries as a "pointer" that directs us toward Him. God is at work all around you, but the physical can cloud the spiritual aspect of life.

We lived in Ohio for several years. One Christmas we were traveling to Alabama to visit our parents. Coming through Kentucky, we ran in to a heavy snow storm. At first it wasn't that bad. But as the snow intensified and began to stick, it became very difficult to see the lanes on the road. To make make matters worse, everything along the road was closed, and I didn't see any motels. As we slowly traversed those Kentucky roads, I could barely make out the tracks of a vehicle that had passed by sometime early. Matter of fact, it was those tracks that kept me in the road. As long as I could follow them, I knew I could stay on pavement and out of the ditch.

Those tracks remind me of those who have come before us. Maybe it was our parents or grandparents. Maybe it was a High School teacher or a Sunday School teacher. But we learn from those who have come before us. Their lives point in a specific direction. Think about King David, Moses, the Apostle Paul, Matthew, Mark, Luke, and John. Their lives point us toward Christ and toward living a life of faith. And in turn, we are pointing those who follow us in a direction. Which way are we pointing? Are we teaching others that life is "all about us"? Or are we teaching others that there's so much more to life "than us"?

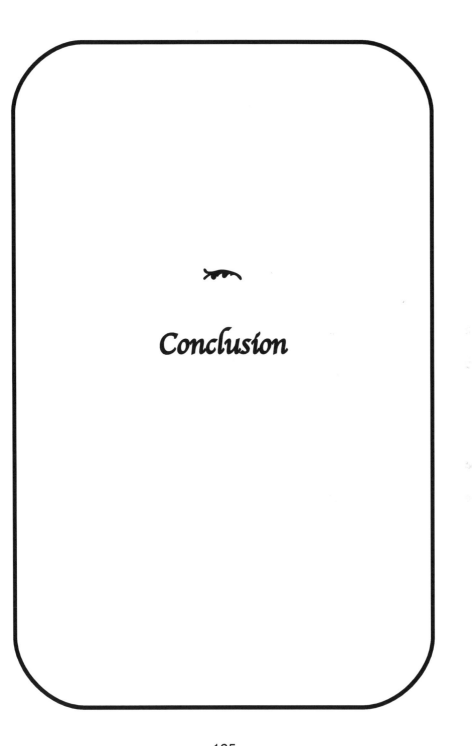

Conclusion

My favorite parable in the New Testament is the story of the talent.
You probably remember the parable well, but we normally don't look at
this story as a story of risk and reward. Matthew tells the story in chapter
25:14-30, "Again,it will be like a man going on a journey, who called his
servants and entrusted his wealth to them. To one he gave five bags of
gold, to another two bags, and to another one bag, each according to his
ability. Then he went on his journey. The man who had received five
bags of gold went at once and put his money to work and gained five
bags more. So also, the one with two bags of gold gained two more. But
the man who had received one bag went off, dug a hole in the ground and
hid his master's money. After a long time the master of those servants
returned and settled accounts with them. The man who had received the
five bags of gold brought the other five. 'Master', he said, 'you entrusted

me with five bags of gold. See, I have gained five more.' His master replied, 'Well done, good and faithful servant! You have been faithful with a few things; I will put you in charge of many things. Come and share your master's happiness!' The man with two bags of gold also came. 'Master,' he said, 'you entrusted me with two bags of gold; see, I have gained two more.' His master replied, 'Well done, good and faithful servant! You have been faithful with a few things; I will put you in charge of many things. Come and share your master's happiness!' Then the man who had received one bag of gold came. 'Master,' he said, 'I knew that you are a hard man, harvesting where you have not sown and gathering where you have not scattered seed. So I was afraid and went out and hid your gold in the ground. See, here is what belongs to you.' His master replied, 'You wicked, lazy servant! So you knew that I harvest where I have not sown and gather where I have not scattered seed? Well then, you should have put my money on deposit with the bankers, so that when I returned I would have received it back with interest. So take the bag of gold from him and give it to the one who has ten bags. For whoever has will be given more, and they will have an abundance. Whoever does not have, even what they have will be taken from them. And throw that worthless servant outside, into the darkness, where there will be weeping and gnashing of teeth.'"

The servants were willing to risk for reward. And the same is true for us. Life's greatest rewards will always come with risk. It's a part of life. What must we be willing to risk? Two things: Resources and time. Time is our greatest resource, and we are only given so much. I heard a really good analogy a few months ago. Time is like a bank account. If the bank called you and said that you would be given $86,400 each day for the rest of your life, you would be happy. What if the bank told you that you had to spend the entire $86,400 by the end of each day, or you would forfeit whatever was left over? If you were like me, you would probably try to spend it. I mean, why let it go to waste? The fact is that we all have such an account called time. We are given 86,400 seconds each day to use. You can have no more – it's exactly 86,400 seconds each day. What's the difference between a money account and a time account? You can't borrow time. You can't take a loan out on your time, or borrow it from someone else. The time you have is the time you have and that's it. Your time is yours to decide, and just like money, you decide how and where you are going to spend it. Here's the thing about time, potential and purpose. God has given you the right amount of time to reach the right amount of potential to fulfill your purpose. You don't need any more time, and you don't need any more potential. It's there – It's yours – to use how you see fit.

Time means everything because it's a gift. I remember going to a bar with some friends one night. I was in my mid-twenties, and enjoyed going out ever so often. Cindy and the kids stayed at home. I walked up to the bar to order a drink, and noticed a middle-aged man sitting alone. He asked me what I was doing there. I guess the question caught me off guard, and honestly made me somewhat angry. I told him I was ordering a drink and asked him what he was doing. The man went on to say that his wife had recently passed away, and he didn't have any family. He asked me again, "what are you doing here, son? Are you married? Do you have kids?" I told him that I was out with some friends for a drink, and that the wife and kids were at home. I felt like a complete idiot telling him – it just seemed so odd admitting that I was at the club drinking while they were home. He said, "man, if my wife and kids were at home – I would be right there with them. They grow up so fast, and time seems to get away from you". I will never forget that conversation. He went on to say, "do you know how you know if you are doing right or wrong? Ask yourself this question: Do you want your kids to grow up being and doing like you are doing now?" I didn't ask the man his name, and I never saw him again after that night. But I do believe that God put him in my path. It made me start thinking. I started to ask myself how I was using my time. Twenty two years later, I still think about that conversation, and I find myself wishing I had some of that time back. What I wouldn't do to go back and change some things. But again, no experience from your past is ever wasted as long as you learn from it. Time is a teacher, and it's up to you what you will learn from it.

For the first twenty years of my life, I thought it was "all about me". I wanted happiness and to have my needs met. I wasn't so worried about the consequences of my actions because I had not really faced many consequences. I was prone to become angry with people and could often be very judgmental. In my thirties, it was all about the family. I wanted to make my wife and children happy. It was all about them. It was all about progressing in my career and providing for my family. Now in my forties, I know that life isn't all about me. And it's not all about my family. It's all about God, and it's all about fulfilling my purpose given to me by God. My purpose has been to be to a good husband and father. My purpose has been to be a good person and to provide for my family. My purpose has been to study and work hard to move ahead in life. But do you know what? That's all secondary purposes. They are all very important in life, but they are not the primary reason for my being. My primary purpose is to realize that life is given by God, and therefore, to know that it is His through both the good and the bad. My purpose is about living each day exponentially. Living, learning and growing through every experience knowing that life has it's ups and downs but also realizing that God is always in control. Life is about "who"?

Life is about God, but God has you and me in mind.

About the Author

Dr. Mark Grizzard has served as a military chaplain, pastor and counselor. Mark served as a special operations chaplain, and later had the opportunity to travel to different bases around the world to speak on Resiliency and Building Healthy Marriages. He is also a presenter for the PREP and Prepare/Enrich inventories. He has served churches in Georgia, Ohio and Florida. Mark currently lives with his family in Helen, Georgia and is a popular speaker at churches and conferences. He enjoys spending time with his family, riding motorcycles, scuba diving, and working out. To contact Mark, check out his website at www.serenityofga.com.

Made in the USA
Columbia, SC
04 October 2024